Peace, Power, and
the United Nations

Peace, Power, and the United Nations

A Security System for the Twenty-first Century

Joseph P. Lorenz

Westview Press
A Member of the Perseus Books Group

Copyright © 1999 by Westview Press, A Member of the Perseus Books Group

Published in 1999 in the United States of America by Westview Press, 5500 Central Avenue, Boulder, Colorado 80301-2877, and in the United Kingdom by Westview Press, 12 Hid's Copse Road, Cumnor Hill, Oxford OX2 9JJ

Library of Congress Cataloging-in-Publication Data
Lorenz, Joseph P.
  Peace, power, and the United Nations : a security system for the twenty-first century / Joseph P. Lorenz.
      p. cm.
  Includes bibliographical references and index.
  ISBN 0-8133-8061-8 (hc)
  1. Security, International.   2. Peaceful change (International relations).   3. United Nations—Armed Forces.   I. Title.
JZ5588.L67   1999
341.5'84—dc21   98-42242
                                                                                  CIP

The paper used in this publication meets the requirements of the American National Standard for Permanence of Paper for Printed Library Materials Z39.48-1984.

10   9   8   7   6   5   4   3   2   1

For Andie and Jeannie, with love

Contents

Acknowledgments

For their help at several stages in the preparation of this book, I am indebted to former colleagues at the U.S. Mission to the United Nations and the Department of State's Bureau of International Organizations, as well as to scholars in the field and my wife and daughters. My special thanks to David Popper, Robert Rosenstock, Samuel Lewis, Michael Newlin, Gerald Helman, Robert Oakley, Inis Claude, and Townsend Hoopes.

I am also grateful to the U.S. Institute of Peace for its financial support, its stimulating seminars and working groups on post–Cold War collective security, and its patience in bearing with changes in the book's focus and subject matter as new threats to peace and security led to new approaches to the use of collective force.

Joseph P. Lorenz

Peace, Power, and
the United Nations

Introduction and Summary

The notion that every state has an interest in the territorial integrity of every other state—no matter how distant they are and how slight their connections—is peculiar to the twentieth century. To be sure, poets and philosophers had perceived humanity's common interest in preventing wars, and statesmen had found that aggression from outside the community could be deterred by the mutual defense of those within it. But no one had ever tried to organize an all-embracing system that used the collective force of its members to prevent one of them from attacking another.

It took the wide devastation of two world wars—and the failure of the balance-of-power systems that preceded them—to instigate the search for a more effective way to manage power. To the founders of the League of Nations and the United Nations there was nothing extravagant about the idea that peace is indivisible. Their countries had been drawn into wars that were largely not of their making: They had learned that to control their destinies they must act early, with others, to keep the peace. It is this core of national self-interest that drives collective security. If the system works at any moment in history, it is because its members believe they have enough stake in the existing order to warrant taking measures against any nation that threatens to destroy the fabric of that order.

The framers of the League Covenant and the UN Charter did not view the systems they were establishing as permanent methods of international cooperation applicable to all power configurations at all times. They were less interested in theory than in the practical problem of managing postwar relationships more systematically than alliance systems had done in the past. The irony, of course, is that both post–world war periods turned out to be very different from what the framers had anticipated, though not too different from what they had feared.

Because of U.S. nonparticipation in the League of Nations and the Cold War's paralyzing effect on the United Nations, the collective-security measures of the League Covenant and the UN Charter have never been applied in the ways envisaged. We cannot be certain if the system's underlying political assumptions are valid or if it can be made to work under certain conditions of power distribution, great-power relationships, developing-world interests, and the like. The chief question at the close of the twentieth century, as in 1918, concerns the willingness of states to participate in military enforcement actions at the direction of others in situations that do not affect their vital interests. There is considerable skepticism that nations will behave in this way but not much analysis of how, and in what circumstances, they might be brought to do so—at least not since the end of the Cold War.

With the breakup of the Soviet Union, a new international order is emerging with its special problems, relationships, and forms of power. How applicable the UN collective-security system is to this new order— and how realistic its assumptions are in a world of competing national interests—is the first of the two main questions this book tries to answer. For these collective-security issues, the U.S.-led enforcement action against Iraq is the principal case study. The second question concerns the steady run of ethnic and factional wars within states, which have emerged as a central problem of post–Cold War politics. Here the UN intervention in Somalia serves as the main case study. The Somalia crisis illustrates the limits of armed intervention in the internal violence that flows from intercommunal antagonisms and the drive for power in failed states. One thread that runs through the book—from the "peace enforcement" operations in Africa to the great-power tripwire missions in the Balkans and the Persian Gulf—is the relationship between consensual peacekeeping and mandatory enforcement action, and the uses of both in regional conflict prevention.

These issues are examined from the viewpoints of history, theory, and practice. Collective security cannot be fully understood without a grasp of its early uses and theoretical roots, and the opening chapters consider the system from these perspectives. (The specialist may wish to skip Chapters 1, 2, and 4, which are designed primarily to provide background for students of international organizations and foreign affairs.) The case studies were chosen for their contemporary relevance, but they also reflect my own familiarity with a number of UN operations from my work on UN peace-and-security issues at the U.S. Mission to the UN and the State Department. That work persuaded me that a modified version of the UN collective-security system, combined with peacekeeping innovations that have evolved since the end of the Cold War, offers increased flexibility in preventive diplomacy, a greater measure of deterrence, and a means of handling secondary threats with secondary responses. In short, it is a way to avoid the all-or-nothing approach to international involvement.

A main line of argumentation in the chapters on collective security concerns the formation of an international deterrent force under Article

43 of the UN Charter. (Issues relating to Article 43, which requires UN members to make designated forces available to the Security Council on its call, are discussed in Chapters 3 and 5.) Any UN force that was established today would look very different from the body the UN's founders had in mind. Changes in the power situation over the last half century would have a major impact on the size, scope, and purposes of a contemporary force. Most important is the change in the nature of the primary threat—from the global expansionism of potential world powers like Germany and Japan in 1945 to the regional ambitions of expansionist middle powers today. Any system intended to contain these regional powers must adjust to two developments in the nature and distribution of modern weapons. First is the huge gap in nuclear and conventional arms sophistication that has developed between the middle powers and the major status quo states. But second, raising the need for an effective system of deterrence to a new level of urgency, is the development of suitcase bombs and anthrax weapons that can be infiltrated into the territory of one's enemies.

Less tangible and subject to shifting perceptions are the changing interests of the major powers, as straight-out threats of aggression have been largely replaced by regional challenges to their economic and political interests. Another change is the nearly fourfold increase in UN membership since World War II, an increase that has occurred mainly through the admission of developing nations, many with a colonial heritage of artificial borders. Finally, the breakup of the Soviet Union has made it possible to think once again about a system for the management of power that rests on the cooperation of the Security Council's permanent members.

My thesis is that these changes open the way to a new kind of UN force that is smaller, cheaper, more realistic in expectations, and more credible in deterrence than the first fifty years of UN history permitted.

The heart of the book, and its principal conclusions, relate to methods of achieving credible deterrence in a collective-security system that stands or falls on deterrence, but now lacks the means to carry out that mission. The proposal that is developed in later chapters for a mobile international deterrent force (or IDF) rests on two premises. The first is that deterrence in today's regional conflicts depends on the capacity to mobilize coalitions of *concerned* states that leave the potential aggressor in no doubt about the identity of the states he will confront and the certainty of defeat. It is no longer necessary, or practical, to establish a worldwide force of such power that it can defeat outright the strongest hypothetical aggressor other than the veto-holding powers, as the Security Council's permanent members believed when they composed the UN Charter.

In these "coalitions of the concerned," the interests of the coalition members will vary from state to state. For the countries of the region, national security interests are likely to be paramount. For the great powers, the motivating concerns may stem from economic or political involvement in the region or from broader issues of global stability. Still other nations may participate because of cultural and religious affiliations with the threatened country. Legal and humanitarian considerations will also play a part, but their effect on national security policy is so uncertain that they cannot now provide the basis of a realistic system for the prevention of war.

The second premise reinforces the first. It is the need for maximum speed in mobilizing a deterrent force *before* the potential aggressor launches an attack. This is precisely what the United Nations cannot do at present. Because of the absence of standby forces under Article 43, the Security Council must rely on ad hoc coalitions of forces that have not trained together and are incapable of rapid deployment. The nations that do have a substantial rapid-deployment capability are the larger Western powers; that is, the countries that have the fewest shared concerns with the participants in most regional quarrels and the least capacity to influence a decision to go to war.

The path to a quick-response capability lies in the negotiation of agreements in which UN members, or groups of members, undertake to form specified rapid-deployment units and keep them in a high degree of readiness. A quick-response capacity would be developed in the major geographic regions, combining highly mobile forces from the area with airlift and special forces units from the major military powers. The permanent members—and other industrial powers like Germany and Japan that have a large airlift capacity by way of their civilian aircraft—would help to form, train, and (in the poorer countries) finance the regional forces. In each area, rapid-deployment maneuvers would be conducted over time by a number of different airlift providers. In this way several major powers would be available to transport regional forces to an area of dispute, depending on the location of the threat, the lift capabilities of the powers participating in the task force, and the relationships between those powers and the threatened states.

A similar flexibility would guide the selection of regional powers for IDF training exercises. If the Security Council is to be able to form coalitions of concerned states, it must have available to it different combinations of regional forces that have trained with the airlift providers. Flexible composition is important to an international deterrent system for two other reasons as well. First is the desirability of combining local powers with their natural allies outside the area. In Southwest Asia, for example, Pakistan and Turkey could be included in maneuvers with conservative Arab nations—the latter participating perhaps as a group representing the Gulf Cooperation Council. Second is the difficulty of combining the culturally and numerically predominant states of an area with an adversary from within the region. In the Middle East, to take the most obvious example, a pragmatic approach to composition might pair the United States, France, or Great Britain with Israel and Turkey in rapid-deployment exercises.

The rapid-deployment units of a deterrent force need not be large. In past UN enforcement actions, the minimum acceptable troop contribution for the smaller participants has been a reinforced battalion. In a deterrent force, some of the rapid-deployment elements could be smaller still. The point is to prevent a war, not to win it; and if deterrence fails, the task of suppressing the aggression falls to the reserve units of the task force in combination with its advance elements. The reserve forces that members agree to make available to the Security Council would be specified in the Article 43 agreements along with the rapid-deployment units. In an international deterrent system, no enforcement action would be authorized unless the combined forces of the coalition, including its reserves, had the ability to defeat the potential aggressor with ease.

Training exercises involving permanent-member forces and the regional rapid-deployment units would be coordinated in the Security Council's Military Staff Committee (MSC), drawing on the experience and personnel of the UN offices responsible for peacekeeping. To keep costs to a minimum, maneuvers would not normally include the reserve elements of a regional IDF deterrent force. In addition to its training responsibilities, the MSC would handle technical matters such as arms standardization and communications compatibility. In this scheme, regional security bodies, assisted by permanent members, would over time perform an increasingly central role in the training of the regional deterrent forces. The Security Council, however, would retain sole responsibility for the authorization and direction of the task forces it established to maintain or restore the peace.

The purpose of a United Nations deterrent system is to provide a flexible response capability for dealing with the two kinds of violence that are most prevalent today. These are cross-border aggression, usually by middle-power military dictatorships, and internal violence in states divided along ethnic or factional lines. The two categories can be further broken down. There is the aggression that threatens important great-power interests and elicits whatever force is needed to suppress it; and there is the aggression against small and poorly armed countries that threatens no one but the victims themselves. Local aggression of the latter kind raises hard questions, often involving a choice between early preventive action by powers with a broad interest in the stability of the region and escalation into wider war.

Like interstate aggression, internal violence also falls into categories that have different implications for international action. There are civil insurrections that remain within the domestic jurisdiction of states and ethnic conflicts that connect with kinship groups outside the state. And there are state-sponsored acts of inhumanity against minorities and random clashes among bandits, warlords, and militias that follow the collapse of states. People disagree on the appropriate responses to these types of aggression and civil conflict. But one thing is clear: The *capacity* of concerned states to mobilize fast-reaction units would widen the foreign-policy choices and provide a flexibility that does not now exist.

For example, in the case of threatened aggression—whether of the unambiguous variety in the Gulf or the indirect and piecemeal version in Bosnia—a number of options become available in a collective-security deterrent system that do not exist without it. First is the tripwire response: the interposition of advance units of the regional task force between the would-be aggressor and the potential victim (as discussed in Chapters 7 and 8). Even if an aggressive intent is not certain, the Security Council has the authority to send forces to the area if it determines that a threat to the peace exists. The council can also declare a military alert to underline the seriousness of a threatened action (as illustrated in Chapter 8). To give the potential aggressor a face-saving exit, it can dispatch to the area a mediation team comprising representatives of the council and the troop-contributing nations. The secretary general can be asked to convey the Security Council's requirements and intentions, as is now the case. And while taking these steps, the council can deploy "over-the-horizon" units of the participating permanent members, whose contributions will provide the ultimate deterrent power in most enforcement actions.

Harder to deal with than interstate aggression are the internal conflicts that ravage some of the world's poorest nations. If the mass murder and starvation inflicted by these conflicts is intolerable to civilized society, no one has yet found a way to relieve the suffering while disarming those who cause it and avoiding the entanglement of those who try to stop it. The chapter on Somalia argues that the best that can usually be done—and it is a great deal—is to provide emergency military transport for the distribution of augmented disaster-relief supplies. Only in the early stages of a deteriorating situation is there much chance of the belligerents in a civil war agreeing to a UN separation-of-forces mission. And the window of opportunity is likely be brief. To take advantage of it, the ability to deploy promptly an observer force whose composition is acceptable to the parties can be crucial. In the Somalia and Rwanda crises, for example, the presence of on-call forces from Africa and the concerned permanent members would have given the Security Council an option it did not have to try to forestall the impending violence.

State-sponsored violations of the Declaration of Human Rights and the genocide convention require different responses from those needed to deal with indiscriminate violence within a failed state. Government crimes against humanity that are so grave in the Security Council's judgment as to require the use of force to stop them cannot be dealt with by peacekeeping or peace enforcement. To suppress genocide or ethnic cleansing, the same capabilities are needed as to defeat cross-border aggression. High on the list is the Security Council's ability to deploy a task force of concerned states with great speed. This is a capability that an international deterrent force could provide in the rare case where permanent-member unanimity (and nonpermanent-member support) overrides the charter injunction against intervention in matters within the domestic jurisdiction of states.

Because the path to an international force already exists in Chapter VII of the UN Charter, the greater emphasis on war prevention would not require charter revision. Indeed, the changes from the early conception of a UN force that a deterrent system entails—greater burden sharing, smaller military and financial contributions, and a strategy of preventive action that reduces the likelihood of conflict—would facilitate the ratification of Article 43 agreements by governments. Even more important to the non-veto-holding states would be a declaration by the permanent members that member states would not be subjected to any requirement to contribute to collective-security operations that were outside their regions and without effect on their interests. Other UN members might, of course, decide to participate for reasons of international law and principle, as substantial numbers did in the ad hoc, after-the-fact enforcement actions in Korea and the Gulf.

If this is a system of lower expectations than the arrangements devised to prevent a third world war, it nevertheless retains essential elements of the UN Charter system. It keeps the responsibility for maintaining the peace with the powers that must bear the burden in human lives and national treasure. It assigns the authority for the strategic direction of UN forces to the permanent members of the Security Council. It locates the command of UN enforcement actions with the participants, normally the permanent member with the largest military contribution. It obligates the members that have concluded Article 43 agreements to participate when called upon in cases involving regional threats to the peace that affect their interests. And its purpose is to maintain or restore international security through the use of adequate force or the manifest resolve to use it. In many of these respects the IDF concept differs from recent proposals for a volunteer peacekeeping force and from other ideas for a powerful, fast-reaction force drawn from the military powers.

The formation of a deterrent force is consistent with the Clinton administration's "Policy on Reforming Multilateral Peace Operations" (PDD 25 of May 1994). First of all, the force would not be "a standing UN army," which the administration opposes. It would consist rather of standby units from which task forces could be formed and tailored to the challenges at hand. (For Europe, a fast-reaction force already exists in the form of NATO's ACE Mobile Force.) The one departure from PDD 25 may be more apparent than real. The document states that the United States will not "earmark specific U.S. military units for participation in UN operations." This stance is based in part on the pragmatic position of the U.S. military that the United States can best support the UN operations in which it participates by shaping its contributions to the nature of the threat.

But the military's opposition to earmarking also reflects its resistance to any action that would supplant combat-readiness training with peacekeeping exercises. In fact, this is a concern that applies more to traditional UN peacekeeping operations than to enforcement actions, which require the same kind of preparedness that is needed to fight and win a war. Still, the high degree of readiness in which U.S. air transport and special forces units are already maintained argues for the U.S. military's position on the ground of fast response time. One path would be for the Security Council to ask the United States to indicate in general rather than specific terms the "numbers and types" of forces it is prepared to make available to an IDF task force whose establishment it supports.

It is clear that an international deterrent system can only be one resource among many in the armory of diplomatic tools needed to fashion a sophisticated foreign policy. It cannot begin to replace U.S. military strength or collective-defense alliances like NATO. It is not applicable to wars that involve the great powers or to most internal violence in failed states. The one overriding national-security purpose of the system is to help prevent regional aggression that threatens the interests of the major powers and the smaller countries that rely on them.

In Southwest Asia, the Middle East, Africa, East Asia, South Asia, and the Balkans, it is easy to identify festering disputes that could erupt into war. If history is any guide, other challenges will come to take the place of those we know today. The most unlikely prospect, as a new century dawns, is a world that is free from threats to the peace and the need for a system to manage them.

1

Collective Security and
Its Antecedents

Early Variations of Collective Security

The first variations on the theme of collective security appeared in the late middle ages, and are instructive for their differences from the twentieth-century concept as well as their similarities to it.[1] These early schemes grew out of the belief that the wars that ravaged Europe during this period could be curbed if all nations agreed to oppose aggression jointly and with overwhelming force. A common thread was the commitment of each state to join in collective action even if not directly threatened. Some of the proposals provided for a council of great-power representatives to determine whether aggression had occurred and, if so, to impose whatever sanctions they deemed necessary. In cases where military measures were decided upon, a multinational force composed of contingents from the European member states was typically assigned the task of enforcing the sanctions.

As much as these ideas resemble the thinking behind the League of Nations and the United Nations, the differences are crucial. The early plans assumed a "we" and a "they," a community of interests, ties, and attitudes that defined itself in terms of its differences from the world outside Europe. The ultimate reason for keeping the peace was to strengthen the Christian community against its enemies. This is apparent in the first comprehensive proposal for collective action, a treatise written by a counselor to Philip the Fair named Pierre Dubois and published in 1306 under the title *The Recovery of the Holy Land*. In this proposal, Dubois recommended that the Catholic sovereigns of the Holy Roman Empire agree to resolve their controversies by arbitration and to act collectively against any one of them that used force in violation of that commitment. But Article 4 of the proposed agreement makes it clear that the object was to promote parochial interests: "The whole commonwealth of Christian believers that owes allegiance to the Roman Church must be joined together in the bonds of peace. . . . If anyone wishes to make war let him be zealous to make war upon the enemies of the Catholic faith, of the Holy Land, and of the places made sacred by the Lord."[2] Dubois's proposal is closer to the collective-defense pacts of the mid–twentieth century than to collective security, differing mainly in its frankness as to who the enemy is and its acknowledgement of the offensive potential of the coalition.

Two other peace plans, among the many that were proposed but not implemented between the fourteenth and eighteenth centuries, illustrate the lack of universality common to all. In 1462, nine years after the fall of Constantinople, King George of Bohemia invited the Catholic sovereigns of Europe to join him in an organization capable of taking collective military action to repel Muslim inroads into Europe. Together the European princes would defend Christianity "against the vilest princes of the Turks [by] joining forces . . . which will be proportionately determined."[3] Similarly, in the early seventeenth century, the Duke of Sully proposed in *The Great Design* a federation of states designed to maintain the security and religious balance of Europe. To enforce the peace he proposed a multinational army and navy that would be used, among other things, "to join to [Europe] such parts of Asia as were most commodiously situated, and particularly the whole coast of Africa, which is too near our own territories for us not to be frequently incommoded by it."[4]

If these early proposals assume a world divided between the Christian states of Europe and the uncivilized realms beyond, they also imply a community of interests in the relationships of the West with Africa and Asia. That sense of common purpose waned during the industrial revolution as economic and political nationalism led to the scramble for overseas possessions. The heightened rivalries among the colonial powers in turn caused these powers to search for new ways to manage European relationships. What emerged was the notion of balancing power among the major powers of Europe—an adaptation of age-old practices of alliance politics to the circumstances of imperialism and the industrial age.

The Classical Balance-of-Power System

As the principal alternative to collective security in the management of interstate conflict, the balance-of-power ideas that had their heyday in the eighteenth and nineteenth centuries shed light on the thinking behind the modern concept of collective security. During and after World War I, when the European alliance system was thoroughly discredited, collective security was designed to replace balance-of-power politics and to be everything the old system was not. During the Cold War the opposite was the case, with alliance politics proclaimed as the realistic successor to utopian plans for universal security through international organization.

Because of the multiple meanings that balance of power has taken on in contemporary usage, it is worth recalling what the concept meant to the European statesmen who developed and practiced it. At the heart of the idea was the principle that the best way to achieve stability in a system of sovereign, competitive nations was to promote an environment in which power was balanced by equivalent power. To work most effectively, the system needed a balancer. Great Britain frequently played this role, especially in the nineteenth century, shifting alliances when necessary to prevent any one European state from becoming strong enough to mount a successful challenge to the status quo. The British managed on the whole to avoid the Cold War tendency to confuse balance with dominance.

The system of decentralized power on which balance-of-power politics depended stemmed largely from the Peace of Westphalia in 1648.[5] Like the League of Nations Covenant and the UN Charter after it, the Peace of Westphalia embodied ideas that responded to a failed system ending in a ruinous, system-wide war. The Thirty Years' War, which led to the Westphalian system, flowed from a medieval feudal order that idealized allegiance to a central authority and left no room for dissent. In reaction, the Westphalian order accepted the sovereign equality of all states in a decentralized world: The objective was not to establish a universal order but to limit the ability of some states to dominate others. What made this more than a utopian dream was the growing ability of the European nations to secure their borders, as the duchies, principalities, and electorates of medieval Europe consolidated into a multitude of defensible states of more or less equal power.

One consequence of the consolidation process was the gradual emergence of a few dominant European powers with a special stake in the system. These nations sought allies with similar interests in order to preserve the status quo and offset the aggressive potential of their likely adversaries. If one of the results from their standpoint was a happy continuation of their preeminence, many of the smaller states saw the system as incapable of righting injustices and accommodating change.

In 1815, after the Napoleonic wars, the Congress of Vienna replaced the laissez-faire approach of the Westphalian world with an international order based explicitly on the principles of balance of power. Embodying this shift toward greater system and design was a new institution for the coordination of great-power interests, the Concert of Europe. The continental powers that made up the Concert of Europe succeeded in shaping a century of relative peace, the longest period of international security that Europe had ever known.[6]

The Concert of Europe was in concept similar to the UN Security Council. Both bodies rose from the ashes of relatively decentralized systems that ended in war, and both were steps toward greater centralization of power. Both were designed to carry out new peacekeeping responsibilities, which the victors had assumed in the expectation that they would cooperate to preserve the postwar order. In the case of the Security Council, it soon became plain that too much had been expected. Yet the habits of consultation that developed in the Security Council and the Concert of Europe limited conflicts that threatened to draw in the great powers. And while the Concert of Europe concerned itself with disputes stemming from the buildup of colonial empires, the Security Council dealt with the quarrels that followed their breakdown.

In the last years before the collapse of the Concert of Europe, new machinery of two kinds emerged that helped shape the international organizations of the twentieth century. First were the "peace conferences" that convened at the Hague in 1899 and 1907. At the 1899 conference, a permanent international court was established to arbitrate "acute conflict[s] threatening to break out between two or more" of the sixteen signatories. No state was obliged to use the court. Its actions, as stated in Article 27 of the Hague Convention, were "only to be considered as an exercise of good offices," and the signatories merely undertook "to remind" the parties to a dispute that the court was open to them. Tentative though they were, these commitments were the source of the voluntary dispute-settlement measures of the League Covenant and the United Nations Charter. In both of these systems, provisions for the peaceful settlement of disputes are part of a sequence from arbitration, mediation, and negotiation to the use of military power. Although the Hague Convention does not deal with the uses of force—and cannot therefore be considered an instrument of collective security—it is a big step toward the collective-security systems of the twentieth century.

At the 1907 Hague Conference, the doors were opened to states from outside Europe. The meetings at the Hague included representatives from forty-four governments, many of them Latin American, and represented the first serious movement toward universality at a peace conference. But formal representation did not translate into an invitation to the corridors of power. The major powers were willing to negotiate uncontroversial issues like codification of the rules of war, but they were less accommodating on issues affecting their own security interests. In other words, these conferences experienced the usual difficulty in achieving a balance between the power of a few nations to enforce the decisions of peace and war and the interest of many in the nature and implementation of those decisions.

The other model for the League of Nations was the network of global unions that grew up in response to the supranational character of modern science and technology. Bodies like the International Telegraphic Union (1865) and the Universal Postal Union (1874) typically included a policymaking congress of all the members and an executive council of limited membership, which met regularly to oversee the implementation of policy. The public unions established habits of businesslike cooperation among a large multinational membership, a pattern that many hoped could be extended to the harder issues of international security.

The Collapse of the Old Order

In seeking the reasons for the breakdown of a century of relative peace into four years of unparalleled devastation, the architects of the post–World War I order focused naturally on the preceding system and its weaknesses. The precise causes of the First World War were far from self-evident, however, and the remedies even less so. The victors put forward three broad, competing explanations for the collapse of the old order. Since all three were addressed by the League of Nations Covenant, a brief look at each may clarify the objectives of collective security as it emerged from World War I.

The first and plainest failure of the old system was the absence of effective dispute settlement machinery. Although states were free to bring their disputes to the Hague tribunal if they wished, the major powers did not use its arbitration procedures in peace-threatening controversies. Moreover, the Concert of Europe, which had sometimes acted as the arbiter of international disputes during the nineteenth century, had fallen into disuse. In any case, by 1914 its members had become more a part of the problem than the solution.

The headlong rush to war in the summer of 1914 persuaded many that the postwar system needed a mandatory "cooling off" period in addition to compulsory dispute settlement procedures. The British and Americans, in particular, believed that mistrust and offended honor had as much to do with the slide to war as real or threatened damage to state interests. The two moving spirits behind the League, President Woodrow Wilson and Lord Robert Cecil, were convinced that with adequate time and the help of an impartial third party, reasonable people could resolve the sorts of disputes that had caused the war. Explaining the League to the American people, Wilson noted that in July 1914 the British had asked Germany and Austria to give the European governments time to confer in order to see if war could be avoided. "It is universally admitted," he added, "that if they had gone into conference . . . the war never would have begun."[7]

The special importance that Wilson and Cecil attached to dispute settlement procedures strongly colored the League of Nations Covenant. In Article 12, at the heart of the peace-and-security provisions that came to be identified with collective security, was the obligation to submit serious international disputes to arbitration and to wait three months before resorting to war. Measures for the peaceful settlement of disputes thus became an integral part of the new system. Yet this Anglo-American view of the League "as an instrument of conciliation, softening all international antagonisms"[8] was fundamentally different from the French approach. It was a difference that was to have serious implications for the future of collective security.

France's perception of the war and its causes was shaped by a half century of jockeying with Germany for European preeminence. After losing the Franco-Prussian War in 1871, France relied on a series of military alliances (mainly with Russia and Britain) to protect itself from a united Germany that had its own treaties with Austria-Hungary and Italy. It was this system of shifting alliances that caused the chain reaction leading to war after the murder of the Austrian crown prince in Sarajevo. To most French, the reason the system broke down was self-evident. Germany and Austria had taken the offensive because the alliance confronting them was not strong enough to make it clear they could not win. At the Paris meetings in 1919, this attitude translated into a renewed French search for security guarantees, broader and firmer if possible than those that had failed to deter Germany before.

The chief purposes of the League, as France saw it, were to enforce the peace treaties and preserve the wartime alliances. It followed that the organization should have a military arm strong enough to turn back challenges to the status quo. Premier Georges Clemenceau proposed that this take the form of either an international army or a multinational force composed of national contingents.[9] In either case, he maintained, an international general staff would be needed to organize the force and direct its operations. Clemenceau also argued for binding decisionmaking power for the new organization to strengthen its peacekeeping capacity.

All of this ran counter to Britain's view that the objective of the League was not so much to perpetuate the status quo as to smooth its rough edges and, as passions subsided, to correct its injustices. Wilson was in the middle. He agreed with the British on the central importance of conciliation. But he also believed that a collective willingness to use force was essential and saw the League as playing the central role in deterring aggression—and, if need be, in suppressing it with force.

After four years of devastating conflict, the British had no intention of guaranteeing the boundaries of countries in which they had no security interest. In the end Wilson compromised, Clemenceau had to go along, and the result was a League that was far more a British "conciliator" than a French "policeman." Constitutionally, this was reflected in Article 10 of the covenant, in which League members undertook to "respect and preserve," rather than "guarantee," the territorial integrity and independence of other members. Article 10 also provided that "the Council shall advise upon the means by which this obligation shall be fulfilled," thus deciding against the French position that the body should have binding decisionmaking authority. In the end, these issues about the wording of the League Covenant had little to do with the causes of World War II: Germany broke specific treaty commitments and none of the Western powers had the political will to oppose it.

The absence of enforcement machinery and central decisionmaking power was aggravated by the exceptionally punitive nature of the peace to which the League of Nations was linked. The territorial transfers, in particular, led to grievances too fundamental to be resolved by mediation or conciliation. And without the deterrence that credible enforcement provisions could provide, the inevitable result was another challenge to the status quo. Ironically, the League probably hastened that challenge by sapping the will of its members to provide for their own defense.

The third, peculiarly American, perspective on the causes of World War I was that the European system of managing power was fundamentally unsound. At bottom this stemmed from contempt for realpolitik diplomacy, a sense that the whole system of shifting alliances was corrupt and needed replacing. Unlike the French and British, Wilson was less interested in tinkering with the old system than in building an alternative to it.

There was evidence to support the Wilsonian view that the balance-of-power system had outlived its usefulness. Two changes in the relationships among European powers played a special part in undercutting the premises of the old order. First, the increasingly rigid alignment of the major powers into two rival blocs removed the flexibility that Britain had provided in its role as balancer. From a system in which the main actors had deliberately fostered an equilibrium to forestall challenges to the status quo, balance-of-power politics had come to mean a situation in which opposing military alliances vied for increased power. At the same time, the competing alliances were engaged in an arms race of unprecedented proportions, which further destabilized the situation.

Wilson described the precarious equilibrium of the period as "one great force balanced against another force."[10] Any member of either coalition, by pressing a quarrel of its own, could trigger the mutual defense provisions of both alliances. In 1914 the controversy between Austria and Serbia was of little direct concern to the rest of Europe. But once Germany and Russia had mobilized in support of the two disputants, the interlocking alliances pulled every major European nation into the war in less than a month. The same system served also to prolong the war, as each alliance member relied on the assurances of the others to continue fighting longer than it might have done had it been without allies.

The second factor leading to the breakdown of the balance-of-power system was the decline of central coordination in European diplomacy. With the great powers' loss of a sense of common interest came increasing neglect of the routine consultations that had helped for a century to prevent major conflict in Europe. In the words of Stanley Hoffmann, a "gradual erosion of the restraints observed by the major actors" had taken place, one of the ways "in which multipolar systems lead to a general war (and balance of power systems are destroyed)."[11]

Just as earlier wars had led to systems of conflict management at the opposite end of a "centralization scale" from the systems preceding them, the structured nature of collective security responded to the failures of the laissez-faire approach. But this time a new element had been added. For the first time, countries from every corner of the globe had been drawn into a conflict that began far from their borders over issues that had little to do with their security. To many it seemed that the interdependence that had widened the net of war required a new form of community action to keep the peace. This notion is embodied in Article 11 of the League of Nations Covenant as the guiding principle of the new system: "Any war or threat of war, whether immediately affecting any Members of the League or not, is . . . a matter of concern to the whole League." Or, as Wilson put it in 1916, the day of the neutrals had passed.[12]

2

Collective Security in the League of Nations Scheme

The Nature of Sanctions Under the Covenant

To the founders of the United Nations, the failure of the League of Nations to prevent the aggression of the 1930s was not so much an indictment of collective security as a result of the major powers' unwillingness to use the system. There was also wide agreement that the League had been seriously flawed by the lack of trained and readily available armed forces. These two defects—the absence of binding obligations and the failure to provide for earmarked military units—were central to the common frame of reference that guided the framers of the UN Charter.

On paper, the sanctions that the League could impose were substantial, although a sharp distinction was drawn between economic and military measures. Economic sanctions were to be imposed automatically on any member that resorted to war in disregard of its obligation to abide by the covenant's dispute-settlement measures. That member, under Article 16 (1), was *"ipso facto* deemed to have committed an act of war against all other Members" and was subject to immediate "severance of all trade or financial relations." Thus the trigger for economic sanctions was not a determination that an act of aggression had been committed or that a threat to the peace existed. Rather, it was the fact of going to war without making use of arbitration, mediation, or judicial settlement procedures and without submitting to a mandatory three-month "cooling-off" period.[1]

Military sanctions, on the other hand, were voluntary. If the covenant's dispute-settlement procedures were disregarded by one of the parties, the League of Nations Council was obliged "to recommend to the several Governments concerned what effective military, naval or air force the Members of the League shall severally contribute ... to protect the covenants of the League." However, any such action not only was advisory but, under the voting provisions of Article 5, required the agreement of all members of the council. In fact, during the twenty turbulent years between the First and Second World Wars, the council did not once recommend the use of force to repel aggression.

Despite the highly qualified nature of the League's provision for military sanctions, the covenant soon came under attack by members wishing to reduce the scope of their obligations. Canada was the torchbearer for nations fearful that a working collective security system would draw them into wars in which they had no state interest. In 1920 Canada moved to strike from the covenant Article 10, the key provision that bound every member to "preserve as against external aggression the territorial integrity and existing political independence of all Members of the League." Three years later, under pressure to preserve at least the kernel of the system, Canada modified its proposal to require that the council "be bound to take account of . . . the geographic situation and the special conditions of each member state" before invoking Article 10.[2] In the end one nation, Persia, voted against the amendment, and the proposal was defeated because of the requirement for unanimity. Nevertheless, the overwhelming skepticism that the debate revealed on the principle that aggression against one member state was to be regarded as aggression against all others was not lost on the revisionist political parties in Europe and Asia.

It is interesting to compare government attitudes twenty-five years later when the issue of mandatory sanctions was discussed at the fifty-nation conference in San Francisco that agreed on the UN Charter. In considering the categorical obligation that was to be incorporated in Article 25 of the UN Charter "to accept and carry out the decisions of the Security Council in accordance with the present Charter," hardly a voice was raised in opposition.[3] In 1945 there was a clear consensus on one point: If every member had the freedom to decide whether to defend a country that was under attack, the response would be ineffective and the deterrence minimal. The remedy seemed to be a clear-cut obligation by every member to respond to aggression with armed force—not when its "geographic situation and special conditions" dictated but when called upon to do so by a body given the primary responsibility for maintaining the peace.[4]

Early Successes in Conflict Prevention

The League of Nations had its successes during the interwar period in spite of the caution of its members, the weakness of its enforcement procedures, the absence of the world's major military powers, and, after 1929, the nationalist pressures of a world depression. Of thirty-nine serious international disputes and conflicts that took place between 1920 and 1939, fourteen were referred to the League. Of these, six were settled peacefully through mediation and conciliation.[5] A number of the League's early interventions bear a striking resemblance to those of the post-Soviet era—in the nature of the disputes, the roles played by the League, and even the cast of characters.

One of the early successes occurred in 1921 after Yugoslavia sent its armed forces into Albania, pillaged Albanian villages, and moved rapidly toward the town of Durazzo on the Adriatic. Acting under Article 11 of the covenant at the request of Great Britain, the council met in Paris on November 16 to decide whether to impose sanctions under Article 16. At the same time, the British House of Commons was debating unilateral measures to avert another Balkan war. Under pressure from Britain and its other European trading partners and in fear of sanctions by the League, Belgrade agreed on November 18 to withdraw its forces and to respect its frontier with Albania. League of Nations representatives accompanied the departing troops to ensure that the council's demands were fully carried out.

In two other conflicts, the League ended hostilities soon after they had begun. In 1925, following a border incident between Greece and Bulgaria, the council secured the withdrawal of Greek forces and the payment of compensation to Bulgaria. Similarly, in a conflict over boundaries between Colombia and Peru in 1932, it arranged a cease-fire and facilitated negotiations between the parties. In this case, foreshadowing UN operations of the future, the League sent a small peacekeeping force to the disputed area in order to ensure the withdrawal of Peruvian troops while the peace talks were in progress.

The most serious crisis of the League's early years occurred after Italy, under Mussolini, invaded the Greek island of Corfu in 1923, sparking a crisis that threatened to spread throughout southern Europe. The council induced Italy to withdraw but could not bring Rome to accept its settlement proposals. The smaller states in the League Assembly severely criticized Britain, France, and other members of the council for failing to apply serious pressure to Italy—although it is not clear what kinds of pressure would have succeeded in changing Italy's policy short of going to war.

Two of the League's successes involved complex ethnic questions similar to those considered by the Security Council since the breakup of the Soviet Union. The first, in 1920, followed a dispute between Sweden and Finland over the Åland Islands, where Finland's legal claim to sovereignty was clear but the islanders themselves had strong ties to Sweden. On the basis of recommendations by a League commission of inquiry and a subsequent convention of concerned parties, Finland was granted sovereignty. At the same time, the islanders were given a large measure of autonomy, and the archipelago was neutralized and demilitarized.

Four years later, the council and the Permanent Court of International Justice became involved in a two-year effort to settle a frontier dispute between Turkey and Iraq, the latter country then under British mandate. Since Turkish border violations persisted after the League became involved, a military investigation team was sent to the area to preserve the status quo while the talks were in progress. The team served its purpose, bringing the military operations to a halt. Less successful were the League's efforts on behalf of ethnic and religious minorities in Turkey. Although the council investigated allegations of Turkish deportations of Christians and mistreatment of Kurds in the Mosul area, it was unable to ascertain all of the facts, much less remedy the situation.

One of the League's more significant achievements was its settlement of the Franco-German dispute over the Saar industrial region in 1935. After World War I France had claimed the territory as compensation for the destruction of its coal mines in the north, even though the inhabitants of the region were almost entirely German. The Paris Treaty granted France a fifteen-year lease on the coalfield (with the administration of the area placed indirectly under the League), after which the local people were to decide their own future. The plebiscite took place in an atmosphere of high tension as Nazi Germany conducted an all-out campaign to prevent the region's transfer to France or its continuation under the League regime.

To ensure a fair and free vote, the League dispatched an international force to monitor the voting. In addition to a special gendarmerie unit to protect the voters, a 3,300-man force of British, Swedish, Italian, and Dutch contingents maintained overall security. On January 13 the voting took place in the Saarland without incident, and the region reverted to Germany in accordance with the overwhelming preference of its inhabitants. The costs of the plebiscite and the security arrangements in the Saarland were borne primarily by France and Germany, the most concerned parties. It is an idea worth rediscovering as the mandates of current, long-standing peacekeeping operations continue to be renewed, removing the parties' incentive for the settlement of intercommunal disputes.

The small, but real, accomplishments of the League during the interwar years share three characteristics. The disputants were either weak countries susceptible to economic pressure or larger powers as yet unprepared for military confrontation; relations among the major powers were still sufficiently businesslike to permit outside conciliation; and none of the conflicts that the League resolved required the use of military force.

Appeasement and the Breakdown of the System

The five cases of Japanese, Italian, and German aggression that led to World War II differed in all three of these respects from the earlier disputes. From Japan's seizure of Manchuria and large parts of China in 1931 and 1937 through Italy's invasion of Ethiopia in 1935 and Germany's annexation of Austria and Czechoslovakia in 1938 and 1939, the aggressors were expansionist dictatorships with little interest in the peaceful settlement of the disputes they provoked. Their military power had reached the point that effective opposition—whether from within the League or outside it—required the threat or use of collective force. And that, in turn, required the kind of major military buildup that none of the Western governments were willing to undertake.

The breakdown of collective security before World War II is not so much the League's story as that of the inward turn of the Western democracies, especially Britain, France, and the United States. The causes of isolationism differed from country to country and are in any event outside the scope of this book. It is worth recalling, however, that the appeasement policies of the period did not ignore the interdependence imposed by modern warfare; on the contrary, they were a response to that interdependence. To many countries recovering from a conflict that had caused 37.5 million casualties from every corner of the globe, neutrality seemed a more credible way to avoid another war than the alliances that had widened World War I or a collective security system that had no teeth.

Like the League Covenant before it, the UN Charter system was an effort to deal with the kinds of aggression and appeasement that had led to a war that was still in progress when the charter was drafted. The challenge-and-response dynamic of the late 1930s helped to shape the UN Charter in several ways. There was first the distinctive nature of the 1930s aggression—its piecemeal, probing quality; its pretexts and disguises; and its goal of territorial aggrandizement. Another characteristic was the power and potential war-making capacity of the revisionist states—all three of them in the early 1930s potential world powers with exceptional industrial and human resources. Last, and related to the first two, was the gradual way in which the vital security interests of the democratic powers became engaged until, finally, the time for deterrence had passed and the only alternative to capitulation was war.

Japanese Aggression and the League Response

Japan's escalating expansion in East Asia was the prototype of this pattern of aggression. The nationalistic elements in the Japanese army and parliament that fomented the invasion of Manchuria in the fall of 1931 had much in common with the fascist regimes that ruled in Italy and soon came to power in Germany. These three middle powers rode the wave of economic hardship and social turmoil that accompanied the worldwide depression. All three also shared a sense of grievance against the Western democracies, inflamed by racist attitudes that created popular support for expansion. And all of them were military dictatorships that dealt with their internal problems through external aggression. None of this was self-evident at the time. On September 10, 1931, eight days before the invasion of Manchuria, Lord Cecil assured the League that "there has scarcely ever been a period in the world's history when war seemed less likely than it does at the present."[6]

Immediately after the Japanese army's occupation of Mukden and other places along the South Manchuria Railway, China invoked Article 11 of the covenant, requesting restoration of the status quo ante and the payment of damages. The council responded with a lukewarm appeal to both sides to refrain from aggravating the situation and to find a means to withdraw all foreign troops. Later, more vigorous efforts to secure a cease-fire and pullback of the Japanese army were vetoed by Japan. Japan's seat on the council also enabled it to buy time by requesting an on-the-spot inquiry before further action was taken. When the resulting commission of inquiry arrived in the Far East in April 1932, Manchuria had been proclaimed an independent state by Japanese collaborationists and Shanghai was under attack. Reporting to the council the following October, the commission condemned Japan for the use of excessive force while scolding China for provocative actions.

Affronted by the council's equivocation, China referred the dispute to the League of Nations Assembly, acting under Article 15 of the covenant. At a special session, the assembly decided unanimously that Japan was the aggressor and called on all members to withhold recognition from the new state of Manchukuo. The principal on which this action was based—the nonrecognition of states created illegally by armed force—was proposed by U.S. Secretary of State Henry L. Stimson. Indeed, Japan's aggression led to a new level of cooperation between the United States and the League of Nations. In the case of Manchukuo, not one member of the League recognized the puppet regime; yet the effect of nonrecognition, far from moderating Japanese expansionism, led to Japan's announcement of its withdrawal from the League of Nations in March 1933.

The events that began with Manchuria and ended with Munich shaped the positions that the United States took on the powers and structure of the United Nations. If Munich represented the European failure to oppose expansionism in its early stages, Pearl Harbor demonstrated the difficulty of defending U.S. Asian interests without peacetime mobilization or binding collective defense engagements. For it was clear that Japanese expansion in Asia could only be stopped by military power—and that in the early 1930s this was not an available option for the United States. Not only did the U.S. Asiatic fleet include no battleships and only one cruiser but the country was totally preoccupied with its domestic economic problems. Similar constraints determined the policies of Britain and France.

Hence the fundamental problem, as perceived by the American drafters of the UN Charter, was to build a system that could prevent revisionist middle powers from acquiring the strength to threaten great-power interests through piecemeal aggression against the weak. The point was not to protect the major military powers from each other—that was their own responsibility. Nor was the UN machinery for the use of overwhelming force devised to keep the peace among the smaller powers, though clearly that would be a result of the system if it worked.

The Italo-Ethiopian War and the Problems of Sanctions

Italy's invasion of Ethiopia in the fall of 1935 led to the League's one serious effort to apply economic measures against an aggressor, and its failure was widely regarded as a lesson arguing for mandatory sanctions. Indeed, the impotence of economic sanctions in the absence of more forceful measures had become so obvious after 1935 that the League was not even a factor in the slide to world war that followed the conquest of Ethiopia. There is a direct line from the Ethiopian crisis to the consensus in the 1940s on the need for mandatory military sanctions to back up economic measures when the latter prove ineffective.

Ironically, however, the League almost certainly would not have invoked binding military sanctions even if the covenant had provided for them because of the appeasement of France, the ambivalence of Britain, and the isolationism of the United States. In December 1934, when Italy began to mobilize after a minor incident on the border between Ethiopia and Italian Somaliland, Adolf Hitler had become the overriding concern in Paris and London. Earlier in the year Benito Mussolini had prevented Hitler's first attempt to annex Austria by a show of force at the Brenner Pass, and at the time he looked like one of the few leaders with the will to stand up to Germany. To Britain and France, Ethiopia seemed a small price to pay for a stable balance of power on the continent.

The League became involved in the Italo-Ethiopian dispute in mid-1935 when Ethiopia, after months of fruitless bilateral negotiations with Rome, requested the good offices of the council under Article 15 of the covenant.[7] The committees set up to mediate the controversy faced a hopeless task, for Mussolini had not the least interest in a settlement. His aim was to consolidate the fascist revolution at home through war, in the process acquiring territory for colonization and raw materials for his "new Roman Empire." The conciliation efforts nevertheless continued through the summer of 1935 while Italy proceeded with a massive military buildup at the Red Sea port of Mits'iwa. The council's report of October 5 absolved Ethiopia of responsibility for the frontier incident and rejected Italian claims. Before the document was issued, however, Italy had launched a full-scale invasion of Ethiopia.

Meanwhile, France and Britain had been struggling with the hard choice of pushing Italy toward alliance with Germany or crippling the collective-security system that depended on their leadership. The two countries responded differently to the dilemma. Throughout the crisis France followed a fairly consistent policy of appeasement, reinforced by political paralysis. In Britain, on the other hand, the government ran into strong opposition as its intention to wink at Italian aggression became apparent. As a result, British policy was erratic and ambivalent. In June 1935, London and Paris tried to arrange the cession of some Ethiopian territory in exchange for an Italian pledge to join an anti-German coalition and refrain from invading the country. Then in August the British and French parted ways as pressure mounted in Britain for straightforward opposition to Italian intimidation. And finally, in September, just before Italy invaded Ethiopia, London led a move at the League in support of Ethiopian independence and territorial integrity.

British vacillation became even more conspicuous after the invasion. On December 9 the British cabinet approved a plan negotiated by British Foreign Secretary Samuel Hoare and French Foreign Minister Pierre Laval surrendering most of Ethiopia to Italy. An outcry arose in Britain over this abandonment of Ethiopia only two months after London had taken the lead in proposing sanctions. Harold Nicolson wrote at the time of the "great indignation that after all this fuss we should be giving Italy more for breaking the Covenant than we offered her for keeping it."[8] In the end the cabinet backed down, Hoare had to resign, and the Hoare-Laval pact was never ratified.

The impact of the economic sanctions against Italy is instructive today as the search continues for a system that can deter aggression without involving its members in the war they seek to prevent. In 1935 most members were prepared to apply a trade embargo and to accept the sacrifices it entailed: Fifty out of the assembly's fifty-four members accepted the council's declaration that Italy was the aggressor and agreed to impose immediate economic sanctions. A consensus soon emerged that the sanctions should include an embargo on arms and essential war matériel, a ban on loans and other financial assistance, and a boycott of all imports from Italy and its possessions.

The sanctions failed primarily because they were subverted by four powers—France, Britain, Germany, and the United States. France sabotaged all efforts to embargo oil, without which the Italian army would have ground to a halt; Britain allowed Rome passage through the Suez Canal, which was essential to the Italian supply line; Germany, no longer a member of the League, happily took up the slack in the sale of arms and other essential commodities; and the United States, driven by economic self-interest, refused to support the embargo in every respect except for a ban on arms shipments to both belligerents. The U.S. position on trade with the belligerents was largely dictated by the Neutrality Acts of 1935 and 1936, which were a by-product of the extreme isolationism in the United States during the 1930s. The Neutrality Acts sought to avoid exposing U.S. merchant ships to submarine attack and, by doing so, to enable the country to stay out of another war in Europe. However, by prohibiting exports to belligerents that were not carried in their own ships, the American legislation effectively precluded assistance to the victims of aggression, not only in Ethiopia but also in China and Spain.[9]

Despite these big holes in the sanctions against Italy, the economic measures that *were* imposed had a powerful impact on the Italian economy. By January 1936 Italian exports had dropped 43 percent from the same period the previous year, and imports had declined 47 percent.[10] It is certainly arguable that the sanctions would have caused Italy to abandon its invasion if the major powers had applied them.

In March 1936, in the midst of the Italo-Ethiopian War, Germany reoccupied the Rhineland, violating both the Treaty of Versailles and the 1925 Treaty of Locarno guaranteeing the French-German-Belgian frontier. The unwillingness of the British and French to meet their covenant obligations in Ethiopia had persuaded Hitler that a direct challenge to France would remain unopposed. (Even so, he assured his generals that the token German occupation force of 22,000 soldiers would be withdrawn if France resisted militarily.) With the Rhineland refortified, further German aggression could no longer be prevented. In the end, the 1930s mixture of realpolitik and halfhearted collective security led to the worst of both worlds. Italy had been driven toward alliance with Germany and Japan; the great powers' unwillingness to apply sanctions in the defense of smaller states had been signaled; and with collective military opposition no longer a credible threat, the only alternative to surrender was total war.[11]

With the withdrawal of the sanctions against Italy in mid-1936 and Japan's invasion of China proper a year later, the League of Nations ceased to be a significant factor in international politics. There were some who regarded its demise as the inevitable outcome of a utopian theory that emphasized legal obligations over the pursuit of national interests conceived in terms of military power. Others, however—among them the leaders who shaped the post–World War II order—saw the League as flawed institutionally but realistic in its principles for the management of power. To them the paramount lesson of the interwar years was that the new organization must be able to keep the peace by force if necessary. Winston Churchill summed up the general feeling in 1939: "When the war is over, we must build up a League of Nations based upon organized force and not upon disorganized nonsense."[12]

3

The UN Charter Approach to Managing Power

Allied Assumptions About the Postwar Order

In considering the relevance of the UN system to the challenges of the post-Soviet era, the first step is to clarify the kinds of threat that the framers of the UN Charter had in mind. Just as the League of Nations was designed to prevent another war by miscalculation, the UN system assumes a threat stemming from the deliberate aggression of expansionist military dictatorships. The intent was to prevent a repetition of the piecemeal aggression of the 1930s by building a structure with the widest possible reciprocal commitments to oppose the threat or use of force wherever it occurred.

The question of the likely source of the next threat had important implications for the structure and powers of the new institution. The only candidates in 1945 were a resurgent Germany or Japan (and, perhaps, a communist China some ten years into the future). It is stretching the point to suggest that the allies were so influenced by retrospective thinking as to devise a system whose only purpose was to deal with the defeated Axis powers. Yet the broad scope of the veto, as agreed at Yalta, led some observers to that conclusion: Harold Nicolson, for one, wrote in April 1945 that "Yalta meant that we should never be able to use the machine against anybody other than Germany and Japan."[1]

The different security interests of the World War II allies became apparent in wartime discussions between Great Britain and the United States on postwar arrangements for the maintenance of peace. Winston Churchill's early preference was for three regional councils, in Europe, Asia, and the Western Hemisphere, preferably with U.S. participation in all three.[2] His objective clearly was to limit British defense obligations to the continent while at the same time committing the United States to the defense of Europe. He phrased this fairly straightforward policy with customary eloquence: "There should be several regional councils, august but subordinate, [and] . . . these should form the massive pillars upon which the world organization would be founded in majesty and calm."[3]

President Franklin D. Roosevelt, on the other hand, believed just as strongly that a small group of major powers should be responsible for policing the world. As the war progressed, Roosevelt came to see the need for greater decentralization of power in a security system whose effectiveness depended largely on near-universal membership. Yet his vision of the postwar order was always closer to the nineteenth-century concert-of-power system than to the decentralized League of Nations structure.[4] Even the "five policemen," who he believed should enforce the peace of the world, were at first two (the United States and Great Britain), then three (after the Soviet Union had driven back the German army), then four (as China was included for strategic and political reasons), and finally five after the liberation of France. Roosevelt's centralized conception of the UN-to-be was shaped in part by his views on disarmament. During the early war years he favored a drastic reduction of arms among the small and middle states, which the great powers would be required to verify and enforce. He realized later that this degree of great-power hegemony so plainly raised the old question of "who is to guard the guards themselves?" that it was unattainable in the real world of sovereign states.

In deference to British and (later) Latin American views, Chapter VIII of the charter bows to regional arrangements, especially in the area of dispute settlement. However, it reserves to the Security Council all collective security decisions, permitting regional organizations to take enforcement action only after the council has given its authority. This decision in favor of centralized authority stemmed largely from the geographical situation and recent experience of the United States.

Japanese expansionism had shown how irrelevant regional institutions were to the protection of U.S. global interests. No Western Hemisphere alliance could have prevented Japan from attacking the United States, much less from expanding in Asia. Senator Arthur H. Vandenberg, the key figure in securing Senate approval of the UN Charter, attributed his own conversion from isolationism to collective security to Japanese aggression: "In my own mind," he wrote, "my convictions regarding international cooperation and collective security for peace took firm form on the afternoon of the Pearl Harbor attack. That day ended isolationism for any realist."[5]

From the beginning, it seemed to the State Department officials who laid the groundwork for the UN Charter that two paths were open to the United States if it was to defend its overseas interests. It could maintain a peacetime military establishment capable of confronting regional aggression before vital U.S. interests were engaged, with the high political and economic costs of such a course. Or it could build a system that included the major European powers and, through preventive diplomacy backed by collective force, discouraged regional powers from the piecemeal aggression that led to World War II.

One point on which the United States and Britain fully agreed was the importance of bringing the wartime coalition into the postwar order. If allied unity could be maintained, the prospect of lasting peace seemed real. If not, and especially if the Soviet Union continued its political and military operations in Eastern Europe, even the best of charters would not make the UN work. There were few illusions about the difficulty of securing long-term Soviet cooperation, but there was no question at all that the attempt had to be made.

The one wartime development that was to have the most far-reaching consequences for the postwar order had little, if any, impact on the charter negotiations. The near completion of the atom bomb was unknown to all but a handful of leaders in the United States and Britain (and, through espionage, in the Soviet Union) when the charter was negotiated in the spring of 1945.[6] There is no evidence that the approach of the nuclear era affected the U.S. or British positions on the charter. Even those who knew how far atomic research had progressed had little conception of the radical change that would take place in the nature of power. And it did not seem likely that any nation other than the United States would be capable of producing nuclear weapons in the near future.[7] Certainly no one imagined that the possession of nuclear weapons by all five permanent members would effectively prevent conflict among them, even while the Cold War barred the way to genuine peace.

The central strategic consideration behind the U.S. effort to ensure Soviet participation in the UN had nothing to do with the coming U.S. nuclear weapons monopoly. When the Dumbarton Oaks conversations opened in mid-1944, the U.S. military had already concluded that postwar cooperation with the Soviets was essential for one overriding reason: The United States would not be able to defeat the USSR in a European land war if the Soviets were to attack Britain after the defeat of Germany. In a letter of May 16, 1944, to Secretary of State Cordell Hull, Admiral William D. Leahy, chairman of the Joint Chiefs of Staff, provided the joint chiefs' assessment of the postwar distribution of power. "In a conflict between [Britain and the Soviet Union]," Leahy wrote, "the disparity in the military strengths that they could dispose upon [the] continent would, under present conditions, be far too great to be overcome by our intervention on the side of Britain. . . . It is apparent that the United States should, now and in the future, exert its utmost efforts . . . to prevent such a situation arising and to promote a spirit of mutual cooperation between Britain, Russia, and ourselves."[8] If the enormous deterrent power of the bomb had been taken into account, it is unlikely that Leahy would have been as concerned about a Soviet attack on Britain.

The disconnection between atomic developments and the charter negotiations is also clear from a memorandum dated April 25, 1945—the day the San Francisco conference convened—from Secretary of War Henry L. Stimson to President Harry S. Truman. Stimson had chief responsibility for U.S. atomic weapons development and was keenly aware of the importance of the new weapon to future world peace. Yet he had no particular suggestions as to how its possession should affect the U.S. position at San Francisco. His memorandum focused mainly on the need for international control: "To approach any world peace organization of any pattern now likely to be considered, without an appreciation by the leaders of our country of the power of this new weapon, would seem to be unrealistic. . . . Both inside any particular country and between the nations of the world, the control of this weapon will be a matter of the greatest importance."[9]

The Soviet Union, for its part, was not only aware of the state of U.S. progress but was developing its own atomic weapons program by 1945. It is possible that Moscow's knowledge of the monopoly that Washington would have for the next few years reinforced its insistence on a more extensive veto right than that favored by the United States and Britain.[10] Whatever the motivation, Soviet demands for the widest possible applicability of the veto were the chief source of controversy among the allies throughout the charter negotiations.

U.S. Domestic and International Security Considerations

The United Nations is, to a remarkable extent, the creation of the United States. Nearly three years of discussion within the Roosevelt administration, and between the administration and Congress, produced a government-wide position on the powers of the UN that was accepted at San Francisco in all of its essentials. Three factors contributed to the deference paid to U.S. views. One was the exceptional military and economic dominance of the United States toward the end of the war, making full U.S. participation essential to the new organization's success. Another was the exhaustive groundwork undertaken by the State Department, leading to U.S. possession of the initiative throughout the negotiations. Finally, broad international agreement on the substance of most of the U.S. positions led to substantial accord on the UN's powers and organization.

For the Roosevelt administration, the overriding lesson of the League of Nations was the need to secure the bipartisan support that had eluded President Wilson. Beginning in 1942, Secretary of State Hull consulted frequently with the Senate and House leadership as State Department planning for the postwar arrangements progressed.[11] Congress, it turned out, was almost as anxious as the administration to avoid the partisan politics that had kept the United States out of the League. As early as September 1943 both houses adopted resolutions supporting U.S. participation in an international organization to ensure "permanent peace," the Senate by a vote of 85 to 5, the House by a vote of 360 to 29. Senator Vandenberg remarked at the time that he considered it essential to "end the miserable notion . . . that the Republican Party will return to its foxhole when the last shot in this war has been fired and will blindly let the world rot in its own anarchy."[12]

In April 1944 Hull arranged for the establishment of a special committee of members of the Senate Foreign Relations Committee (known as the "Committee of Eight") to consider informally draft proposals that were being developed for discussion with the British. The committee consisted of Democrats Tom Connally, Walter George, Alben Barkley, and Guy Gillette; Republicans Arthur Vandenberg, Warren Austin, and Wallace White; and Progressive Robert La Follette Jr. The administration's consultations with this committee and other influential members of the Senate and House were not an exercise in protocol; indeed, they examined some of the hardest questions of sovereignty-limitation and war-making authority that collective security raises for democratic states.

The central issues in the consultations with Congress concerned the uses and limits of collective force. They included the source of authority for military sanctions, the circumstances in which enforcement actions would be launched, the great-power veto, and the preservation of the constitutional responsibility of Congress in the declaration of war. Fifty years later some of these questions have yet to be answered. And since the United States, now as then, must take the lead if the collective security system of the UN Charter is to be implemented, the positions of the administration and Congress on these issues during the war are of continuing interest.

Great Power Concert, Collective Security, or Both?

The UN Charter's approach to conflict resolution can be seen as part of the historic tension between centralization and decentralization in the management of power. Roosevelt, as we have seen, was at first a proponent of extreme centralization. Cordell Hull, on the other hand, was the most consistent advocate of a system of collective security tempered by the lessons of the League. Hull's influence suffered from the president's tendency to act as his own secretary of state. On the other hand, it profited from Roosevelt's preoccupation with the conduct of the war, from Hull's excellent relations with Congress, and from the State Department's formal responsibility for postwar security planning. Hull also got help from an unexpected quarter. In August 1944, Republican presidential candidate Thomas E. Dewey declared that he was disturbed by reports that the forthcoming talks at Dumbarton Oaks were intended to "subject the nations of the world, great and small, permanently to the coercive power of the four nations holding this conference."[13] Hull replied that these fears were "utterly and completely unfounded," grateful perhaps that Dewey's concern helped to make them so.

Governor Dewey's statement also started a chain of events that ended in one of the most notable cases of bipartisan foreign-policy cooperation in U.S. history. On August 23, in response to Hull's invitation, Dewey asked John Foster Dulles to work with the administration in keeping politics out of the peace arrangements. The consultations that followed helped to avoid misunderstandings with the Republican leadership and to reinforce the bipartisan course that Hull had already charted with Congress. Dewey later commented that the charter negotiations raised only one important foreign policy issue: "the use of armed force by the proposed security organization."[14]

Hull believed that the new system would stand or fall on the willingness of the great powers to use collective force to keep the peace. In a December 1943 memorandum to the president, transmitting a draft plan of the new organization, he stated his reasons:

> The entire plan is based on two central assumptions: First, that the four major powers will pledge themselves and will consider themselves morally bound not to go to war against each other or against any other nation, and to cooperate with each other and with other peace-loving states in maintaining the peace; and . . . second, that each of them will maintain adequate forces and will be willing to use such forces as circumstances require to prevent or suppress all cases of aggression.[15]

The basic thrust of the memorandum—not that the major powers would necessarily cooperate but that the new system would not work unless they did—became the guiding principle behind the U.S. approach to the negotiations on a charter for the new organization at Dumbarton Oaks and San Francisco. The mechanism for great-power cooperation was to be the Security Council; and although the council had a more acceptable title than "the five policemen," it was a direct descendent of the consortium of overwhelming power that Roosevelt advocated.

Congress and the Hard Questions of Sovereignty

Because of the ineffectiveness of the League of Nations voting procedures, which provided for unanimity in the council and voluntary compliance in the assembly, the need to delegate to a small body the authority to invoke sanctions was an essential element of U.S. planning. The
difficult questions were (1) whether the affirmative votes of all of the permanent members should be required for the Security Council to act and
(2) if so, on what kinds of issues. The overall size of the council was also a
significant early issue; however, it was soon recognized that size had little importance if the permanent members retained the right of veto.

In the earliest draft of the charter, prepared by the State Department in
August 1943, the council was to include the four allied powers (the
United States, Britain, China, and the USSR) and three other states
elected for annual terms. At this stage, the prevailing department view
was that decisions should be made by a two-thirds majority vote, including three-fourths of the permanent members.[16] The principal argument
against four-power unanimity was that it might drive away some of the
smaller states whose participation was essential to an organization based
on universal membership. They would have a good case since the two
great wars of the century had not been caused by them but by the major
military powers.

On February 3, 1944, Roosevelt settled the veto question, at least with
respect to the use of armed force. He declared that the interests of the
"Big Four" required their unanimity on "the most crucial matters," emphasizing that the United States must not be called upon to furnish
armed forces without its consent.[17] The president's decision reflected two
major concerns: (1) the importance of continued great-power cooperation
and (2) the need for Senate agreement to U.S. participation. By early 1944
the State Department had concluded that a veto-less system could lead to
dangerous confrontation among the major powers. Hull told Roosevelt
that nothing was more likely to provoke another world war than an effort by one permanent member to impose mandatory military sanctions
on another. He added that the supposed advantages of more democratic
voting were illusory: There was simply no way of making a permanent
member contribute to an enforcement action against its wishes.

Although important differences were to arise with the Soviet Union
over the veto's scope, the United States would from this point on be a
steadfast supporter of the veto in all decisions involving the possibility of
enforcement action. With Congress in particular, the veto was portrayed
as a U.S. initiative. In May 1944, for example, while discussing a draft UN
charter with a group of senators, Hull declared that the veto was in the
charter "primarily on account of the United States."[18]

Hull conducted his most intensive consultations with Congress during the spring of 1944, chiefly through the Senate "Committee of Eight." (The service chiefs were also formally consulted at this stage, although military representatives had already been participating informally in the discussions chaired by the State Department.) The Committee of Eight did not accept the principle of great-power unanimity as readily as might have been expected. Senators Gillette and Austin worried that the veto gave too much power to the less responsible members of the "Big Four."[19] Vandenberg was unwilling to agree in advance to an organization that, like the League, might be called on to uphold peace agreements that were unjust. He was especially concerned that the UN might end up sanctioning the Soviet Union's incorporation of independent states and Britain's preservation of its colonial empire. On the whole, however, Vandenberg was favorably disposed toward the U.S. draft. "The striking thing about it," he wrote, "is that it is so *conservative* from a nationalist standpoint. . . . No action looking toward the use of force can be taken if any one of the Big Four dissents."[20]

During the year ahead, after the U.S. plan became public, Congress strongly supported the administration's position on the veto. At San Francisco, for example, Senator Connally made it clear that the veto was the price of U.S. ratification. To his fellow delegates he declared that "they could vote to kill the veto if they liked, but there would be no United Nations if they did."[21]

If the veto was the most widely discussed issue during the planning stages of the charter, another problem arose during Hull's consultations with Senate leaders that was equally charged with questions of sovereignty and constitutionality. This was the matter of reconciling the power of Congress to declare war under the U.S. Constitution with the new organization's need to react quickly and forcibly to aggression. The consensus that was reached on this issue was reflected in the UN Participation Act of 1945 and remains U.S. law. It has two main elements: (1) Congress will approve any agreement between the Security Council and the United States on the nature and size of the U.S. forces to be held on call for use by the council, and (2) Congress will, in addition, authorize the use of U.S. forces in every case where the prospective deployment exceeds the numbers committed under that agreement.

The path to this solution would be traveled again if a decision were made to activate the collective-security provisions of the UN Charter. When the issue of congressional approval was first raised by Senate leaders in the spring of 1944, Hull gave his assurance that any agreement with the Security Council would be submitted to the Senate for approval. The issue surfaced again on August 25 at a briefing of congressional leaders on the Dumbarton Oaks discussions, which were then taking place with

Great Britain and the Soviet Union. Perhaps having tested the waters in the Senate, Vandenberg took a harder position at this briefing. He maintained that congressional approval must be obtained even before the deployment of U.S. forces earmarked for Security Council use, at least in some cases.[22] Hull took strong exception. He argued that such a practice would run counter to the fundamental purpose of collective security: to deter aggression by ensuring that the response is immediate, automatic, and sufficient to the task. A half century later, immediacy, sufficiency, and automaticity—to the extent that they are practical and politically acceptable—are still the hallmarks of an effective collective-security system. The international deterrent force proposed in these pages is an effort to come as close as possible to these goals in the post–Cold War power situation.

The controversy over the war-making powers of the legislative and executive branches continued along familiar lines for a few more days, then disappeared from sight as a major issue. Vandenberg alarmed Hull at this time by writing that a U.S. vote for military sanctions in the Security Council seemed to him "tantamount to a declaration of war," a power that he reminded the secretary was assigned by the Constitution to Congress, not the executive.[23] Hull countered with a State Department legal memorandum on the right, and practice, of the president to take military action when required without a declaration of war. Vandenberg accepted the point, recognizing that the issue went to the heart of the new organization's effectiveness.

The other question concerning the role of Congress was whether an agreement with the Security Council on the provision of U.S. forces should be considered a treaty requiring approval of a two-thirds majority of the Senate. The Senate Foreign Relations Committee explored the issue in 1945 when the UN Charter was under consideration. Dulles told the committee that the agreement on the size and scope of the U.S. contribution should require a two-thirds majority, and the comments of the senators indicate broad agreement with this position.[24]

If the problem of legislative approval is a difficult one for the United States, it is far more troublesome for states that do not hold the veto. Among these states, Canada has been the most consistent exponent of the notion that members have no obligation to contribute earmarked forces to UN operations that do not affect their national interests. In 1944, as in 1920, it tried to reserve the right to approve or deny any Security Council deployment of its troops. At a meeting on September 4, 1944, Lester Pearson, the Canadian ambassador to the United States, said as much to Alexander Cadogan, the British representative to the Dumbarton Oaks negotiations. "Bless my soul," Cadogan said, "if we put in such provisions, the world will say, 'Where are the teeth you promised to put in the Covenant? We are back where we were before.'"[25]

At San Francisco, Canada and other middle powers settled for the right of a potential troop contributor, before being called on to provide armed forces, "to participate in the decisions of the Security Council concerning the employment of [its] contingents." This provision now appears in Article 44, embodying what the Netherlands delegate at San Francisco called the principle of "no military action without representation."[26] Article 44 is rarely mentioned in discussions of UN collective security. But it is a significant dilution of the "automaticity" of the obligation to contribute to enforcement actions on the call of the Security Council. In its effect it is not much different from the Security Council declaration suggested earlier in connection with the formation of an international deterrent force (IDF): namely, that member states would not be subjected to any requirement to contribute to collective-security operations that were outside their regions and without effect on their interests. The further dilution of "automaticity" that takes place in the process of putting together a UN collective-security force is discussed in Chapter 8 in connection with the ad hoc enforcement action in the Persian Gulf.

If the Security Council undertook to negotiate the special agreements that are called for in Article 43, the issue of parliamentary consent would doubtless be revisited by UN members with representative governments. If that occurred, the U.S. position would again set an important example. It might well be concluded that the balance of interests now reflected in the UN Participation Act is as reasonable a compromise as can be expected.

Key Issues at Dumbarton Oaks, San Francisco, and Yalta

Earmarked Contingents or Standing Army?

Among the architects of the charter, there was no early consensus on whether the new international force should be a standing army or a body of earmarked national units on standby status. Both arrangements had their advantages. Indeed, each of the Dumbarton Oaks participants favored a permanent force during some stage of its policy development.[27] It seemed self-evident that a standing army would be able to respond to aggression faster than on-call units, that it would require less time for consultations on the composition of each operation, and that joint training would simplify the problems of logistics and command. At the same time, it became clear at San Francisco that a standing army—particularly one of the great size and power being contemplated at the time—involved limits on sovereignty that were unacceptable not only to the permanent members but to the smaller states as well.

In addition, the military establishments of the major powers did not look kindly on the transfer of their best-trained and equipped units to an international command. Admiral Leahy recorded the U.S. military's opposition to a standing force in a memorandum of March 28, 1944: "To maintain . . . a denationalized, integrated force as a military entity on an effective footing," he wrote, "would involve serious technical difficulties."[28]

Although the issue was settled at San Francisco in favor of standby forces, it has continued to receive intermittent attention. The Kennedy administration, for example, considered the possibility of creating a permanent UN force in connection with the policing of a general disarmament agreement. And in the late 1990s, as a quick-response capability becomes central to military effectiveness in regional conflicts, it is still necessary to reconcile the U.S. military's need to keep special forces units at peak readiness for national-defense purposes and the Security Council's need for rapid-deployment units to respond to urgent threats to the peace.

Great-Power Differences over the Veto

The Dumbarton Oaks talks convened in the summer of 1944 with the participation of the United States, Great Britain, and the Soviet Union. (Nationalist China was relegated to a second "conference" with the United States and Britain at the insistence of the USSR). Before long a complex dispute arose over the scope of the veto, which not only divided the allies among themselves but later pitted them against most of the rest of the world. The issue on which the talks deadlocked was whether a permanent member should have the right to block Security Council consideration of a dispute to which it is a party. The Soviet position alone was consistent throughout the Dumbarton Oaks discussions and the six months that followed. The Soviets favored an absolute right of veto at every stage of Security Council consideration, even if a permanent member was involved and the proposed action called for recommendations for peaceful settlement rather than decisions on enforcement action. The United States and Britain took different positions at different times, depending partly on whether great-power unity or equal application of the charter was the dominant consideration of the moment.

These questions remained open until the February 1945 tripartite summit at Yalta, where Roosevelt and Churchill persuaded Stalin to drop the absolutist Soviet position on the veto. The Yalta voting formula claimed no veto right on the *consideration* of disputes under the peaceful-settlement provisions of the charter. Further, the three allies agreed that a permanent member directly involved in a dispute must abstain from vot-

ing if the Security Council decides to make recommendations for its settlement. This understanding was later incorporated into the UN Charter
as Article 27 (3).

At the UN conference in San Francisco from April 25 to June 26, 1945,
the United States, Great Britain, and the Soviet Union stood firm against
efforts to further limit the scope of the veto. In a joint statement of interpretation, the permanent members responded to a list of twenty-seven
questions that other delegations submitted on the veto's applicability to
specific situations. At the heart of that statement is a justification of the
right of veto in disputes to which no permanent member is a party: "Beyond this point [the point at which the council decides to consider a dis-
pute], decisions and actions by the Security Council may well have major
political consequences and may even initiate a chain of events which
might, in the end, require the Council under its responsibilities to invoke
measures of enforcement under [what came to be Chapter VII]."[29]

With the benefit of hindsight, it seems clear that the allies were right in
insisting on a voting system ensuring that the Security Council could
adopt no decision that might start a chain of events leading to war between the great powers. Indeed, the founders wrought better than they
knew. The approaching combination of Cold War rivalry and nuclear-
weapons development was to underscore the urgency of avoiding such a
confrontation. The veto protected the superpowers from themselves. It
helped both of them resist the temptation to use surrogate states for military action against each other. Korea, as we shall see, was the exception
that proved the rule to big and small powers alike.

Chapter VII: Consensus on a New Enforcement System

The collective-security provisions of the charter—the muscle and sinew
of the UN system of power management—are set forth in Chapter VII,
"Action with Respect to Threats to the Peace, Breaches of the Peace, and
Acts of Aggression." The most striking aspect of these far-reaching provisions is the limited controversy they provoked while the charter was being drafted. It is true that some of the hardest problems were yet to come,
among them the nature and size of the permanent members' contributions to a UN force. That, however, is a story that belongs to the postwar
Military Staff Committee talks, which are discussed in Chapter 5.

Although the key provisions of Chapter VII will be considered later,
they can be briefly summarized:

Article 39 provides that "the Security Council shall determine the
    existence of any threat to the peace, breach of the peace, or act of
    aggression and shall make recommendations, or decide what

measures shall be taken in accordance with Articles 41 or 42, to maintain or restore international peace and security." This article overturns the guiding principle of the League of Nations, that "it is the duty of each member to decide for himself whether a breach of the Covenant has been committed" (League of Nations Resolution 4, interpreting Article 16).

Articles 41 and 42 stipulate the kinds of economic and military sanctions that the Security Council may employ to give effect to its decisions. These articles provide for binding decisions by the Security Council on a wide range of graduated measures that may be applied to maintain or restore international peace.

Article 43 requires that all UN members "undertake to make available to the Security Council, on its call and in accordance with a special agreement or agreements, armed forces, assistance, and facilities, including rights of passage, necessary for the purpose of maintaining international peace and security." Article 43 is the linchpin of the UN Charter. On its implementation hinges the council's capacity to prevent and suppress aggression through its recourse to overwhelming, rapidly deployable collective force.

Article 47, paragraph 3 governs "the strategic direction of any armed forces placed at the disposal of the Security Council," assigning that responsibility to a Military Staff Committee comprising the chiefs of staff of the permanent members and serving under the authority of the Security Council. By "strategic direction" the framers of the charter meant the military planning and direction of large multinational operations, as distinguished from tactical command on the one hand and political control on the other. The concept of such a committee flowed directly from the Combined Chiefs of Staff of World War II, whose planning of the allied campaigns was a major factor in the successful conduct of the war.

The Secretary General's Authority in the Uses of Force

In 1945 the United States shared with virtually all UN members the view that the secretary general was the "chief administrative officer of the Organization," as Article 97 puts it, and not much more. The only security function that the charter confers on the secretary general is the right to "bring to the attention of the Security Council any matter which in his opinion may threaten the maintenance of international peace and security." These words from Article 99 clearly do not envisage any responsibility for the direction and command of UN enforcement actions. Yet Article 99 adds to the political importance of the office by giving its incumbent the discretion to raise matters that the Security Council might prefer to ignore. As used by Dag Hammarskjöld in the Congo and by Boutros Boutros-Ghali in his reproof to the Security Council for "not lifting a finger to save Somalia," it can be the voice of a suffering people who have no other advocate. It can also generate wide popular concern and compassion, and thereby *become* an interest and concern of the Security Council members.

Ever since the UN's earliest years, there has been controversy over the secretary general's authority in peace-and-security matters. During the Cold War, Washington was the champion of broad authority for the secretary general in the conduct of peacekeeping operations. For fifteen years, from the election of Trygve Lie to the untimely death of Dag Hammarskjöld in 1961, the United States could count on secretaries general who, while independent in character, acted in accordance with Western values. The most significant example occurred in 1950, when Lie called for urgent UN action to counter North Korean aggression, angering the Soviet Union and prompting it to oppose his nomination for a second term.

Earlier, foreshadowing a proposal by Secretary General Boutros-Ghali in 1992, Lie had suggested "the establishment of a comparatively small guard force, as distinct from a striking force, recruited by the Secretary-General and placed at the disposal of the Security Council."[30] This recurring proposal, as discussed in connection with the UN intervention in Somalia, is inconsistent with the Security Council's responsibility under the charter for all important matters relating to the management and control of force. Even in peacekeeping (or "guard") missions, the size and composition of a force can be important in dealing with the political and military problems that arise during these operations. The proposals of Lie and Boutros-Ghali received no support from the permanent members (including the United States, despite its professed preference for "independent" secretaries general) and, indeed, very little backing from the membership as a whole.

In 1960 the East-West controversy over the secretary general's powers led to the most serious crisis in the UN's history. The immediate cause was Secretary General Hammarskjöld's independent direction of the UN Force in the Congo, and specifically his support for an anti-Soviet faction in the struggle for power, over the fierce opposition of the Soviet Union. The result was the Soviet Union's refusal to pay its share of the costs of the 20,000-man operation, leading to a huge UN deficit and one of the major confrontations of the Cold War.

After the Congo operation, in an effort to reconcile the positions of the superpowers, the General Assembly set up a Committee on Peacekeeping Guidelines to draft principles governing the authority of the secretary general in peacekeeping operations. The committee never did agree on the guidelines. The failure of this enterprise, however, did not interfere with the effective conduct of the peacekeeping missions of the Cold War. Indeed, it may have helped the process by enabling the superpowers to accept a pragmatic division of responsibilities for each peacekeeping force without appearing to sacrifice their respective principles.

The UN Charter in a Changing World Order

The road to San Francisco ended on June 25, 1945, with the unanimous adoption of the UN Charter by fifty nations whose principal link to each other was association in the still unfinished war against the Axis. These wartime confederates expected different things from the new organization, depending on whether they were weak or strong, rich or poor, democratic or authoritarian, revisionist or protective of the status quo. And although they shared the goal of preventing a third world war, not one of them would have ratified the charter if the UN had seemed to conflict with its vital national interests. The unanimous acceptance of the charter is all the more remarkable as the document does not, for the most part, paper over differing interests with generalities, as did the League of Nations Covenant. On the contrary, it provides for mechanisms and obligations that modify sovereignty in ways that had been unthinkable twenty-five years earlier.

A number of elements contributed to the consensus at San Francisco beyond the obvious need for compromise if the major powers were to participate in the new organization. An important consideration was the flexibility of the charter itself, with its alternative approaches to dispute settlement and its provision for graduated responses to threats to the peace. This flexibility has been demonstrated repeatedly over the years and is central to the UN's ability to adapt to the power arrangements of the twenty-first century.

If the UN Charter is conservative in providing for the continuing dominance of the allied powers, it is in other respects remarkably forward looking. A clear shift took place from the emphasis in the League of Nations Covenant on European security toward greater focus on the developing world's place in the maintenance of peace. Writing during the Cold War, Inis Claude makes the point with characteristic felicity: "The Charter was decidedly futuristic. . . . Indeed, a case can be made for the proposition that the creators of the United Nations suffered from abnormal foresightedness—that they visualized more clearly, and thus made the new institutional system more appropriate to deal with, the potential causes of World War IV than the probable causes of World War III."[31]

Several charter provisions deal specifically with developing-world concerns. For example, Articles 55 and 56 pledge members to take "joint and separate action" for the achievement of human rights and other fundamental freedoms. Indeed, the whole of Chapter IX reflects the insight that human rights, economic development, democracy, and international security are inextricably linked. Long before the Security Council authorized interventions in Iraqi Kurdistan and Somalia for humanitarian reasons, the founders recognized that individual and minority rights were of international concern.

The small and middle powers are also guaranteed a significant voice in peace-and-security decisions under the voting provisions of Article 27. In the enlarged, fifteen-member council, which came into being in 1965,[32] Article 27 provides that "decisions of the Security Council . . . [on all nonprocedural matters require] an affirmative vote of nine members including the concurring votes of the permanent members." Put another way, seven of the ten nonpermanent members, acting together, can block a decision backed by all of the permanent members. Further, as a practical matter, developing nations currently have an effective veto over most decisions that they oppose as a group because of China's unwillingness to act against a united Third World position.

Geographic distribution also comes into play in Security Council decisions. At the time of the 1965 enlargement, the General Assembly formally fixed the regional distribution of the nonpermanent member seats. Five are to be elected from African and Asian states; one from Eastern Europe; two from Latin America; and two from Western European and other states (such as Canada and Australia).

Since the adoption of the UN Charter, the membership of the United Nations has almost quadrupled, the decolonization process has ended, the Soviet Union has ceased to exist, and nuclear weapons have fundamentally altered the nature of war and the characteristics of power. One might suppose that these changes would require extensive charter revision, if not a different system entirely. In fact, the experience of fifty years has shown that the UN Charter, like the U.S. Constitution, is capable of adapting to changing interests and needs so long as there is a consensus on what they are and what should be done about them.

4

Collective Force Theory and National Power

For forty years the United Nations led a double life. As superpower competition replaced the allied cooperation of the war years, the UN's two main bodies reacted to the bipolar power structure in different ways. Over time, the Security Council put into practice a whole new peace-keeping system that served to lessen the possibility of great-power conflict in areas of East-West confrontation. The General Assembly, lacking operational responsibility for security issues, turned increasingly to theater. It provided the stage for the Cold War morality play, where the perfidy of one's adversaries could be exposed and the righteousness of one's own policies proclaimed to a global audience.

Current thinking on the role of collective power in the post-Soviet order is discussed in the case studies on the Gulf war and Somalia. This chapter considers a legacy from the Cold War years: four decades of scholarly work on the issues of balance-of-power and collective-security theory. Cold War theory continues to be relevant. It shaped the outlook of a generation of scholars and practitioners, whose views developed during World War II and its aftermath and whose work laid the foundation for contemporary thinking on the issues of collective force. Also, because of its emphasis on balance-of-power politics, Cold War theory points out the similarities and differences between collective security and its main alternative.

Power Maximization as the Basis of Foreign Policy

The specialists in international affairs who came to the fore after World War II had a different view of the world from their predecessors. Bringing order to the world community seemed a less rational enterprise than it had been before the war. The collapse of the League of Nations through fear and appeasement, the world's descent into anarchy through racism and nationalism, and the brutality of the war itself—all had eroded confidence in international laws and institutions. Between the interwar and postwar generations, a fundamental change had taken place in the premises of political theory. The crucial difference, in Clement Attlee's view, was a change of expectations: "I belong to the generation which believed that the world was more or less settled, that it had become to a greater or less extent civilized, but many of you here were born into a world in which you expect constant trouble—and get it."[1]

The effect of these changes was to move the emphasis of foreign policy analysis from international law and organizations to the sphere of national interest and power.[2] From the scrutiny of covenants and agreements, the focus shifted to an examination of the underlying forces that shape national behavior. The obligations of the UN Charter seemed less important to an understanding of international politics than the power context that produced them. The leading proponent of this view, Hans J. Morgenthau, wrote in 1945 that "international treaties of a political nature derive their meaning not from their text alone but from their text in conjunction with the political considerations which gave rise to them and which continue to determine their functions for the relations between nations."[3]

At the heart of Morgenthau's balance-of-power theory is the proposition that politics is "the concept of interest defined in terms of power."[4] The nature of national power therefore becomes the central question. Morgenthau's conception of power and its component parts is restrictive, starting from the premise that power, in every era, can be defined only in national security terms. And that, in turn, leads to the insistence that foreign policy cannot concern itself with spheres of action that are unrelated to strategic power. Among these excluded spheres of action are "economics (understood in terms of interest defined as wealth)" and international law.[5]

In Morgenthau's system, every nation has its own special power requirements—an "objective national interest" residing in its own security needs. The point is elaborated by Kenneth W. Thompson, a follower of Morgenthau and fellow exponent of the school of "political realism." Thompson emphasizes the geopolitical nature of these objective national interests. "Rational foreign policy," he writes, is driven by "a clustering of strategic interests ... [arising from] geographic position, historic objectives, and relationship to other power centers."[6]

The theme was further developed by Nicholas J. Spykman, a contemporary of Morgenthau whose special interest was the impact of geographic position on international power arrangements. Spykman argues that national boundaries will inevitably move whenever pressures between states become unequal. "At any given time, there are some [states] that are satisfied and others that are dissatisfied with the political and territorial status quo. When such dissatisfaction reaches a certain point, efforts will be made to change the situation by force."[7] Every nation must therefore concern itself primarily with the preservation and improvement of its power position, for no "other method than the use of force [can be] found to protect [its] security."[8]

One may agree with Morgenthau that international politics is the concept of interest defined in terms of power, while disagreeing with the view that power can be defined only in strategic terms. A preoccupation with the national-security component of power leads to an overly simplified view of world politics. While it reminds us to look for the hard interests that underlie the most "principled" of foreign policies, it takes insufficient account of nonstrategic elements, particularly personal and power elite–based domestic interests. And in the late twentieth century, any theory that neglects the predominance of economic interest over strategic power in democratic, industrially advanced nations misses an important element in the relationship between national power and foreign policy.[9]

The Morgenthau school also misreads the relationship between national interest and political morality. The relationship is not one of interest *over* morality but of interest, rightly assessed, *as* morality. Political morality lies in the soundness of a leader's judgments about the strategic, economic, and diplomatic interests that are appropriate to a nation's well-being at a given time. As domestic priorities change and the distribution of power shifts, the national interest may lie in revising the status quo or preserving it, in augmenting military power or contracting it, in emphasizing domestic economic reform or neglecting it for an assertive foreign policy.

Collective security, no less than the balance of power, is driven by the pursuit of national interests, as distinct from the interests of supranational groups or organizations. Whatever their nature at a given time, these national interests are almost always subject to serious limitations. Even at the height of the Cold War, the restraints that the superpowers imposed on their global competition were as central to world politics as the competition itself. Perhaps the clearest modern illustration of a foreign policy based on the limits of armed force rather than its uses is the U.S. approach to East-West relationships during the Cold War known as containment.

Limits on the Pursuit of Power:
The Case of Containment

Faced with a new, and imperfectly understood, threat of military expansion and political subversion after World War II, American opinion coalesced around three views of the Soviet challenge and what to do about it. Broadly speaking, the three perspectives emphasized the ideological, military, and political characteristics of Soviet foreign policy. Advocates of the three schools engaged in a running debate on the principles of international politics. Thus, while Morgenthau was emphasizing the dominance of power politics in response to the ideological character of early U.S. Cold War policy, George F. Kennan was developing the doctrine of containment to refute the militaristic view of the Soviet threat.

Kennan's doctrine of containment is one of history's most sophisticated and successful policies for the management of international power. It is also an instructive variation on the balance-of-power theme, even though balance-of-power theorists tend to claim Kennan as one of their own.[10] A comparison of containment policy with balance-of-power theory reveals fundamental differences between them as well as similarities.

The most obvious similarity is that both concepts seek a power equilibrium in order to deter aggression and fix the boundaries of great-power competition. Both look to national interest as the guidepost of a rational foreign policy. And both take aim at similar targets: the Cold War moralists and militarists on the fringes of public opinion and national security policy. In his landmark 1947 essay on U.S. policy toward the Soviet Union, Kennan warns against exaggerating the ideological aspects of the Cold War, noting that "the containment of Russian expansionist tendencies . . . has nothing to do with outward histrionics."[11] A decade later, still emphasizing the primarily political character of Soviet expansionism, he criticizes the "overmilitarization of thinking in the West on the nature of the Soviet threat."[12]

Despite the similarities, Kennan's approach differs from balance-of-power theory on fundamental issues of method and substance. Cold War balance-of-power doctrine claims derivation from general principles of world politics, notably the fixed and definitive role of strategic power in international relations. Containment policy, to the contrary, is based on judgments about the *limits* of power politics—in particular, the limits of Soviet expansionism imposed by the pursuit of unlimited domestic authority.[13] Its distinction lies in its profound insights into the foreign policy implications of Russian history, Soviet politics, and the East-West distribution of power.

Kennan's national interest is a house of many mansions, made up of different domestic and foreign interests that change over time. The same premise is implicit in collective security. Collective security assumes that every nation has secondary security needs as well as vital strategic interests, which can best be pursued by sharing the economic and military costs with others. Also implicit is the assumption that economic prosperity and social justice must compete with national security for scarce resources and that security is not necessarily entitled to priority. Kennan goes further. Throughout his writing over a period of fifty years, one thread reappears: International power and leadership depend primarily on the economic, social, and moral health of one's own country.[14] "The real competition [with the USSR]," he writes in 1957, is to "see which of us moves most rapidly and successfully to the solution of his own particular problems, and to the fulfillment of his own peculiar ideals."[15]

In spite of its "city-on-a-hill" connotations, Kennan's political theory is far from isolationist but is rooted instead in the notion of balance between internal and external pressures. Though conscious of the limits of one state's capacity to affect the behavior of another, it is attentive to the opportunities for advancing political and economic interests abroad. It is impatient with abstractions, skeptical of the view that progress is inevitable, sensible to the limitations and needs of one's own country, and concerned about the effects of injecting self-righteousness into foreign policy.[16] On these premises, and on a careful reading of history, Kennan built as realistic a foundation for the conduct of foreign relations as has ever driven U.S. policy.

Balance-of-Power Responses to New Forms of Power

Of the three systems for the management of power that have been urged in the twentieth century—collective security, balance of power, and world federalism—the only remaining alternative to collective security is balance of power. Unlike world-government theory, the balance-of-power concept survived the Cold War, even if its advocates do not always agree on what it means. Balance of power can mean (1) a policy of confronting power with countervailing power, (2) a situation of balance in one state's favor, or (3) the simple pursuit of increased power.[17] But the term also refers to a coherent strategy of preventing war through the creation of a power equilibrium, and it is in this sense that it is used here.

Traditional balance-of-power theory, as noted earlier, seeks a distribution of power in which no state or group of states has the military strength to challenge the status quo. To achieve this distribution, the system needs a balancer—a power that deliberately shifts its weight among a group of potential contenders to prevent one or more of them from achieving hegemony. The system has other characteristics as well. It requires that the balancer be prepared to follow a fluctuating, morally neutral foreign policy. It assumes that the actors in the system are relatively small in number and of comparable strength, as in nineteenth-century Europe. And it is driven by the balancer's own interest in the avoidance of conflict.

During the Cold War, great-power interests and relationships differed in important respects from these assumptions. Whereas the traditional system depended on flexibility and ease of movement between rival blocs, the Cold War world was notable for the rigidity of its alignments. The balance could change, but only by one superpower increasing its power at the expense of the other or drawing uncommitted nations into its orbit. What emerged was a pattern of direct opposition, each bloc striving to see its policies prevail until war or capitulation decided the outcome. As Morgenthau himself points out, a balance of direct opposition is inherently unstable. It cannot fulfill the main function that "the balance of power is supposed to fulfill . . . [that of] stability in the power relations among nations."[18] In sum, in its Cold War usage, the term "balance of power" makes sense only if used in a way that is directly contrary to its original meaning describing a power situation in which two competing blocs strive for a preponderance, or *imbalance*, of power.

As applied to the post–Cold War world (for here we must anticipate), balance-of-power theory has suffered an even greater sea change. Clearly no longer applicable to great-power relationships in a world of nuclear standoff and U.S. military dominance, the strategy is applied now to regional conflict management. The United States has become the principal balancer, the world is the stage, and the balances are to be determined by the calculations of outsiders rather than by the judgment of the balancer on how to align itself to avoid war.

Today's balance-of-power proponents argue that in strategically important regions, the United States should seek to maintain a power equilibrium without regard to moral preference. In the Persian Gulf, for example, Henry Kissinger has argued that the United States should treat Iraq as part of the long-term balance with Iran, Syria, and other regional powers instead of "branding [it] as forever beyond the pale."[19] As the old balances in Europe and Northeast Asia come apart with the collapse of Soviet power, he maintains that the United States should act as balancer, with its allies where possible, to shape a new equilibrium.

Balance-of-power theory is not so easily transplanted from its original setting. Managing the power relationships of Asian and Middle Eastern states is more difficult than transferring allegiances within a small group of familiar European powers. Even if U.S. leaders had the exceptional insights into regional-power intentions, military strength, and internal politics needed to conduct successful regional balance-of-power policies, foreign and domestic pressures would make it hard for them to do so. In the Gulf, for example, strengthening Iraq's position to balance Iran would lead to requests from Israel and its supporters for new arms to balance those provided Iraq, followed by pressure from Egypt and Saudi Arabia to balance the weapons given to Israel.

These problems are aggravated by the race of the industrial powers to arm rival states in precisely the areas where military balance is most needed. The would-be balancer has the formidable task of persuading arms suppliers not only that its judgment about the nature of a stable balance is sound but that, on the basis of that judgment, they should give up their hard-currency earnings from weapons sales.

A more practical and stabilizing approach to regional balance is area-wide arms limitation, negotiated by the countries of a region and their major suppliers. This path is linked to collective security in two ways. First, the regional parties to such agreements are likely to insist on credible assurances of security after their weapons have been limited—assurances that a working collective-security system could provide. Second, the lower the levels of arms that have been agreed to, the more effective collective security can be in preventing and suppressing regional aggression.

Post–Cold War changes in the arrangements of power have altered the political landscape in ways that are fundamentally incompatible with the premises of balance-of-power theory. Collective security, on the other hand, wholly unsuited to a world of bipolar competition, has emerged as the basis for a realistic, interest-driven approach to international order.

Implications of Weapons of Mass Destruction for Collective Security

Greatly complicating balance-of-power theory over the past five decades has been the development of nuclear, chemical, and biological weapons of mass destruction. The "balance of terror" that resulted from the assured devastation of both superpowers in a nuclear exchange imposed unheard-of restraints on the use of military force by one great power against another. In Raymond Aron's phrase, a nuclear power might be able to retaliate after a nuclear attack, "but its reprisal would be, so to speak, posthumous."[20] In the early 1960s Aron argued that nuclear weapons had made stability part of a triad of strategic concepts, along with deterrence and arms control. He saw the search for stability as "replacing the old notion of balance of power in providing the theoretical basis for assuring that the great-power rivals do not resort to the forces at their disposal."[21] Winston Churchill also viewed the nuclear standoff as a substitute for balance-of-power politics. He went so far as to suggest that "the universality of potential destruction . . . [may be looked at] with hope and even confidence."[22]

Nuclear weapons have also helped to prevent the escalation of conventional wars, especially in strategically important areas like the Middle East. As Henry Kissinger put it, "the necessity of avoiding a nuclear holocaust" increased the interest of the great powers in limiting the quarrels of the middle powers that could draw them into conflict with each other.[23] Although this interest has become less compelling with the passing of the Cold War, the use of force along historical lines, for conquest or expansion, remains unthinkable for the first-rank nuclear powers, and almost so for the second-rank nuclear powers.[24] For many people who live in the poorer, autocratic states of the world, this is cold comfort. Moreover, it is important to distinguish between the restraints on the uses of force for external expansion and the absence of such restraints in internal conflicts. In the latter, as Stanley Hoffmann writes, "force in the nuclear age is still the 'midwife of societies' insofar as revolutionary war either breeds new nations or shapes regimes in existing nations."[25]

Most Cold War political theorists take the view that nuclear weapons lessened the relevance of UN collective security. "Who can imagine," Inis Claude asks, "that a contemporary superpower, brandishing his fiendishly powerful modern weapons, could be deterred from aggression by the threat of the United Nations to improvise a collective military venture?"[26] Walter Lippmann makes a similar point: "When there are bombs so powerful that one of them can knock out a small country, and two or three of them can subdue a middle-sized state, the main assumptions of collective security are wiped out. Small countries within the reach of a nuclear power are not likely to join hands in war against it."[27] Never mind that the veto was designed to exclude the permanent members from sanctions even before nuclear weapons became a factor: The authors are clearly right that collective security has no place in a situation of relatively equal power distribution between two armed camps.

The elimination of the offensive military option for the Security Council's permanent members has transformed the nature of the compact between them and the other members of the United Nations. At San Francisco in 1945, the most troublesome aspect of the UN system for most states was the permanent members' exemption from military sanctions by their possession of the veto. As it turned out, the problem took care of itself, as self-preservation compelled the great powers to avoid the use of force against each other and their allies.

Collective Security and Its Critics

Despite collective security's unsuitedness to the Cold War order, the most intensive study of the system took place in the 1950s and early 1960s. Several of the most influential political theorists of the period had been present at the creation of the UN and remained interested in the conditions under which the system might be made to work. The requirements, as they saw them, fell into two broad categories: the objective conditions, in the sense of great-power relationships and the distribution of power, and the subjective needs, in the sense of popular attitudes toward national interests and sovereignty. This is a convenient framework for a discussion of the political requirements of an effective collective-security system as seen by some of its most thoughtful critics, among them Raymond Aron, Walter Lippmann, Henry Kissinger, and Inis Claude.

Distribution of Power Requirements

The ideal setting for a pure and veto-less system of collective security, most political scientists agree, is a world characterized by a substantial diffusion of power.[28] Since the central premise of collective security is that potential aggressors will be deterred by the prospect of certain defeat when confronted by overwhelming force, it follows that the most effective deterrence flows from the widest distribution of power. For example, if the world's strongest nation commands 15 percent of the resources of power, the remaining 85 percent should in theory be available to suppress aggression from any quarter. In this power configuration, no member of a universal collective-security organization would have to furnish more than a small portion of its armed forces to create an insuperable international force, even allowing for some members' nonparticipation. The relatively low level of sacrifice required of each nation would add credibility to the threat of collective action.

Desirable as it may be in theory, a widely diffused distribution of power was no more characteristic of the world in 1945 than it is at century's end. It is precisely because power was concentrated in a small number of major states that the UN system owes as much to the concert-of-power experience as to collective-security theory. Article 51 of the UN Charter, which affirms "the inherent right of individual or collective defence if an armed attack occurs" until the Security Council can act to restore the peace, reflects two basic assumptions about the power distribution after World War II. The first is that great-power aggression can be prevented only through traditional military alliances, the second that doctrinaire collective security risks turning local conflicts into global wars. These two assumptions remain valid, for if great-power cooperation is needed for collective security to work, the veto is needed for those times when that cooperation no longer exists.

The Implications of Universality

The League of Nations experience showed the importance of great-power participation in a collective-security system; what is not so obvious is the need for lesser-power participation in the economic and political sanctions that drive collective security. In economic sanctions, little is easier than the subversion of a trade embargo by countries seeking the opportunities for high profits and new markets that accompany the inter-ruption of economic relations. In Italy, North Korea, and to a lesser extent Iraq, a small number of states were able to undermine the economic sanc-tions of the majority.

Military sanctions also rely for their effectiveness on the willingness of the small and middle powers to contribute armed forces and facilities. There is usually a critical moment in the chain of events leading to armed conflict when aggression seems probable, but not yet certain. It is at this point that the Security Council must be able to let the would-be aggressor know which member states will be called on to put down the aggression if it occurs. Only if the council has readily available to it mobile forces from the powers of the region, as well as from permanent members, are its warnings likely to be credible.

The UN's long march toward universality, even during the discord of the Cold War, is one of the most significant developments in its history, with implications that extend beyond the requirements of collective secu-rity.[29] It is hard now to credit the extraordinary amount of time and emo-tion that went into the divided-states membership issues. No other set of problems so polarized the General Assembly as the annual Cold War confrontations over Chinese representation and Korean membership.[30] The disappearance of these issues from the agenda is one reason for the more businesslike atmosphere that characterizes most UN proceedings today.

Consensus on the Status Quo: The Case of Russia

For the Security Council to function as the primary instrument for the maintenance of peace, a minimum consensus must exist among the per-manent members on the territorial arrangements that are to be pre-served.[31] So long as the communist and nonaligned blocs challenged the legitimacy of the Cold War territorial arrangements, there was no hope of forging a consensus against violent change. Russia's inward turn since 1987 has opened the door at least to the kind of cooperation among the permanent members that the framers of the UN Charter saw as the indis-pensable condition to a working collective-security system.

The interests that have driven Russia's UN policy since 1987 have not changed. The need to divert resources from the military to domestic con-sumption and economic restructuring remains compelling. And the suc-cessful pursuit of a more open society and a market economy continues to depend on aid from the industrial powers and, eventually, partial eco-nomic integration with them. These interests dictate a cautious foreign policy, a stable world order, and the Security Council's continued preem-inence in security matters.

Under Mikhail Gorbachev, the Soviets worked in a number of ways to strengthen the collective-security mechanisms of the charter. Speaking to the General Assembly in September 1990, for example, Eduard A. Shevardnadze, then Soviet foreign minister, declared that the USSR was prepared to negotiate an agreement under which Soviet forces would be made available to the Security Council in accordance with Article 43 of the charter. He made it clear, however, that Soviet participation in enforcement actions would be subject to parliamentary approval, a significant qualification in view of the aversion of the parliament and the people to the use of force for strategic purposes in the post-Afghanistan, post-Chechnya era. Russia will doubtless continue to try to have it both ways, supporting UN actions that preserve its great-power status while avoiding participation in measures that divert resources from domestic needs.

After World War II, as will be discussed in the next chapter, the permanent members accepted their participation in collective-security operations as an integral part of the UN system. Indeed, they agreed that, initially at least, they should provide the major portion of an overall UN standby force. Today, Russia's interests are more complicated. On the one hand, the more spectacular the fall from superpower status, the more urgent is Russia's need to protect its position in the Security Council. Permanent membership and the veto compensate for Russia's weakness and allow it to play a global role. At the same time, enforcement action poses serious dilemmas for Russia's leadership: Major participation diverts resources from domestic needs while second-rank participation involves sensitive problems of status and influence. The question is whether these contradictions, and similar ones affecting China, can be reconciled to permit the participation of these powers in UN enforcement actions.

The participation of all five permanent members would be essential to the effectiveness of the collective-security deterrent system described earlier. Unless the permanent members are ready to train an international deterrent force and participate in IDF task forces when their interests are engaged, the other members will not negotiate the Article 43 agreements, on which the system rests. Also, credible deterrence depends on the assurance that at least one permanent member will participate in every UN enforcement action. Russia and China must be a part of the system if it is to work. The surest way to bankrupt a security system for the twenty-first century is to expect the Western permanent members to assume a disproportionate share of the burden.

If pressed to agree in principle to participate in the deterrent task forces that they vote to establish, Russia and China might find it hard to refuse. A commitment of this kind would not affect their right to veto operations they oppose; both must protect their status as permanent members and their relations with the major Western powers; and the extent of their participation would depend on the degree to which a conflict threatened their interests. In an international deterrent force, permanent-member contributions would often consist mainly of over-the-horizon strategic forces in support of the interested states of the region. The task forces would be so overwhelming in such situations as to ensure that combat would be avoided or aggression quickly defeated.

Several of the former Soviet republics pose a special problem. Complications are bound to arise over the UN's peacemaking and peacekeeping role in these states when violence erupts. In one case, they already have. In August 1993, in the conflict between Georgia and the secessionist region of Abkhazia, Russia asked the Security Council to send a substantial UN force to calm the situation. Fearing an effort by Moscow to reimpose its control, the Western members put off the decision for a year and then agreed to send only a group of 136 observers.

As history moves forward and new power elites appear with different ideas about their countries' needs, the interests of Russia and other major powers will change again. Nonetheless, while it lasts, the great-power consensus in favor of stability offers an opportunity to expand areas of common concern, ingrain habits of peaceful settlement, and build the institutions needed to cope with the conflict-management problems of the future.

The Third World's Interest in the Status Quo

Russia's preoccupation with domestic issues has its counterpart in a greater emphasis on economic development in much of the Third World. The change from the climate in the UN's early and middle years is striking. Then, the struggle against colonialism was the main concern of new Asian and African members, and peacekeeping was often seen as a Western device for freezing the status quo. The different atmosphere of the late 1990s is apparent in the swing from confrontation toward cooperation in the General Assembly, most notably in the assembly's repeal of the Zionism-racism resolution in late 1991.[32]

Once the decolonization process came to an end, so also did the driving ideological force behind forty years of confrontational politics in the UN. At about the same time, a new generation of leaders with a stake in the international order came to power. Concerned with the practical problems of nation building and faced with the bankruptcy of the confrontational politics of the Cold War, these leaders look to the United Nations for practical assistance. This means aid in coping with economic difficulties and environmental problems, but it also means help in keeping the peace so that scarce resources can be used for development instead of defense.

The Heart of the Sovereignty Problem

The prospects for a collective-security system at any given time depend largely on the prevailing attitudes toward sovereignty and the uses of force that are associated with it. These attitudes vary from one period to another, from the absolute and independent authority of the state in the mid–nineteenth century to the strict limits on unsanctioned force that the war-weary nations of the world agreed to in the summer of 1945. They vary also as national interests change, as political systems become more or less democratic, as peaceful alternatives for the achievement of national objectives develop, and as (and if) the costs of aggression come to outweigh its benefits.

There are many who believe that the concept of sovereignty-as-absolute-authority is too integral to the nation-state system to accommodate the assumption that nations will employ force to suppress aggression when their direct interests are not at stake. They regard UN collective security as unrealistic in the two major constraints that it places on independent action: first, in the positive obligation to provide armed forces when called upon even if the aggression poses no threat to them (Article 48), and second, in the negative obligation to refrain from the threat or use of force against the territorial integrity or political independence of any other state (Article 2 [4]). When sovereignty considerations conflict with collective security, these critics argue, the former will always prevail. The modifications to the present UN system that underlie the IDF proposal are an attempt to deal seriously with these concerns. Let us consider the principal sovereignty arguments as they relate to collective security.

Henry Kissinger argues in his first major work, in 1957, that sovereignty considerations make a worldwide system of collective security extremely difficult to implement. "The essence of sovereignty," he writes, "is that powers have, or at least *may* have, different conceptions of their interest and, therefore, also about what constitutes a threat."[33] Because of these differences, he maintains, a global consensus on the question of whether a particular use of force represents aggression and, if so, what form resistance should take, is difficult to attain on all but the most overpowering threats. "Against any other danger, united action is almost inevitably reduced to the lowest common denominator . . . [for a] state will not easily risk its national existence to defeat an aggression not explicitly directed against its national existence."[34]

This is not only an eloquent expression of the most common argument against collective security but a clear statement of the most common flaw in that argument. There is nothing in the UN Charter, the negotiations surrounding it, or the statements of the 185 states that have accepted its obligations that suggests a requirement to risk one's national existence for a cause that does not threaten that existence. UN collective security does not rely on self-immolation but on negotiated agreements that commit a small part of each member's armed forces to the pool of collective power.

Like Kissinger, Walter Lippmann concludes that collective security is feasible only as a last resort, when the fate of nations is at stake. "The trouble with collective security," he argues, "is . . . that when the issue is less than the survival of great nations, the method of collective security will not be used because it is just as terrifying to the policeman as it is to the lawbreakers."[35] In point of fact, the survival of great nations is the one task for which collective security is least suited. The veto exists to prevent the UN system from being used by one permanent member against another in disputes involving national existence and survival. To protect those vital interests, the self-defense provisions of Article 51 were drafted and the collective-defense alliances of the Cold War were formed.

In considering the relationship between collective security and sovereignty, Raymond Aron points to two areas of potential conflict. One is "the essential anarchy" of the sovereign state system, "which never has been, nor can be, eliminated, because there is no authority above states that has the means to restrain them."[36] The other is the unreality of the assumption that states will fight for anything other than the defense of their own short-term security interests. "The difficulty [with collective security]," Aron writes, "is simple. A state can be restrained only by the threat or use of force. And since nations that are not directly concerned are loath to go to war for reasons of law or morality, why should a great power yield to an international community that is unwilling to employ force?"[37] Here again, as with Lippmann, the argument suggests that collective security is designed to counter great-power aggression. It is a premise that can be understood only in the outdated Cold War context of overriding Western preoccupation with the threat of Soviet direct or indirect aggression.

The heart of the sovereignty problem for the UN system lies in the credibility of its members' commitments to make agreed-upon forces available to the Security Council when called on to do so. Clearly the makeup of these coalitions would vary from one threat to another, normally combining troops from the regional powers with the greatest interest in local stability with forces from the major powers with the greatest stake in global stability. Deterrence lies in this combination of global and regional power.

The UN system does not depend on the participation of states that have no interest in a dispute; it does depend on the willingness of its members to contribute to the pool of forces that must exist if coalitions of the concerned are to be quickly formed when threats to the peace occur.

These global/regional-power coalitions have different sovereignty implications for the permanent members and the regional powers. For the world powers it would seem at first glance that the issue does not even arise. A permanent member can no more be compelled to vote for an enforcement action than it can be restrained from using unilateral force if its interests are threatened. Nevertheless, the protection of the veto must be balanced by the *perception* that a system for the use of collective force must inevitably limit independent action. There is no doubt that the perception is correct. A working collective-security system would, through the evolution of accepted practice over time, almost certainly limit the unilateral use of armed force in cases other than self-defense. And that, of course, is the point of the system.

For states other than the council's permanent members, the obligation to contribute to enforcement actions at a hypothetical time, in hypothetical circumstances, against a hypothetical aggressor may be a disturbing prospect. And yet there are real-life reasons to believe that UN members as a whole would hardly be more likely to serve in UN operations against their will than the permanent members. For one thing, the voting arrangements of the council are such that the smaller powers, as a group, have a veto over peace-and-security actions that are supported by the major powers alone. For another, enforcement actions that fail to attract the principal regional powers are unlikely to be pressed, since they lack the advantages that the UN umbrella provides: legitimacy, universal application of economic sanctions, military burden sharing, and the aggressor's isolation from neighbors and natural allies. Finally, there is not much that can be done to make a UN member serve in an enforcement action that it opposes. In the ad hoc collective-security action against Iraq, for example, the Western powers presumably did what they could to persuade Jordan to join the UN coalition, with no success at all and with little discernible effect on Jordan's relations with the West.

Yet it would be a mistake to conclude from this that the second- and third-rank powers would not take part in IDF task forces. The UN's experience with peacekeeping has shown a more disinterested willingness to take part in hazardous operations than might have been expected. In some of the more dangerous actions, like those in Lebanon and Somalia where casualties were almost certain, a large and geographically diverse group of small and middle powers contributed troops, presumably in part because they consider UN collective action to be in their long-term interests.

Limits on the Use of Collective Force in Democracies

In the advanced democracies, collective security encounters a special set of attitudes and emotional responses that are often at cross-purposes with each other. On the one hand, democratic states do not, as a rule, initiate large-scale wars; they are the classic status quo powers on which a collective-security system must rely. On the other hand, the aversion that most people have to risking their lives without compelling reasons can make the democratic nations uncertain partners in a collective-security system. The shifting sands of public opinion affect the predictability on which collective security rests. Democracies cannot always do what a collective-security system requires with the speed that it requires; the nature of the threat must first be understood and public support developed for the response.

Alexis de Tocqueville pointed out a special paradox in the attitude of the American people toward the use of force. He believed that democratic societies in general, and the United States in particular, are inherently peaceable. At the same time, he forecast that once a war began the United States would have great difficulty ending it: "When a war has at length ... roused the whole community from their peaceful occupations ... the same passions that made them attach so much importance to the maintenance of peace will be turned to arms."[38]

There are those who believe that the answer of a democratic people to UN enforcement action will always be No, no matter how convincingly the threat and the response are explained. Among the most pessimistic is Lippmann. "On momentous issues," he writes, "the only words that a great mass ... can speak [are] Yes or No. ... In matters of war and peace the popular answer in the democracies is likely to be No. ... At the critical junctures, when the stakes are high, the prevailing mass opinion will impose what amounts to a veto. ... Prepare for war in time of peace? No. Intervene in a developing conflict? No. Avoid the risk of war."[39] This assessment is overdrawn. When the national interest is clear, the objective achievable, and the response proportionate to the threat, the democracies do not have a bad record of doing what has to be done.

Is collective security, then, incompatible with the claims of sovereignty and the conditions of democracy? If not, under what circumstances would the UN be able to carry out the peace-and-security tasks that the founders asked of it? "Would it be enough," Aron asks, "to change certain elements in the situation, or would it be necessary to change the essential characteristics between states as we have known them for the past six thousand years?"[40]

Although Aron does not answer directly, the question prompts him to make some perceptive comments about the conditions for collective security. First is the general observation that there is little point in speculating about *any* system of international politics that is not firmly rooted in the sovereign right of states to defend their interests, of which they alone must be the final judges. Second, with respect to the specific "elements in the situation" that would have to change for the UN to function as intended, Aron sees two changes as critical. One is that the Security Council must be able to reach agreement in recognizing "the unqualified aggression by a state . . . in designating it as such, and . . . in calling upon the Member States" to come to the aid of the victim.[41] The other is that the conflict must "lend itself to the legal formalism of the Charter so that the wrongs of the parties may be determined . . . by reference to the . . . fundamental concepts" on which the UN is founded.[42]

Here Aron may be exaggerating the importance of "legal formalism." One of the UN's major strengths is the recognition by its founders that effective joint action derives from the political interests and judgments of the Security Council and other concerned UN members. The General Assembly conceded as much in Resolution 3314 (XXIX) of December 14, 1974, which reflects agreement on a definition of "aggression" after years of North-South and East-West controversy over the term. The preamble of the definition states that "the question whether an act of aggression has been committed must be considered in the light of all the circumstances of each particular case."[43]

In his most comprehensive work on international politics, *Paix et Guerre entre les nations,* Aron adds another, overarching requirement for collective security:

> It is necessary that the [great powers] . . . be determined to uphold the status quo, whatever it may be, or at the least to view the actions of the parties to a conflict equitably and impartially. . . . States must feel themselves sufficiently interested in maintaining the juridical order to accept the risks and ultimate sacrifices that may be necessary to defend an interest which is not, strictly speaking, national, but which is nevertheless *their* interest over the long run.[44]

Few would assign such sweeping importance to upholding the status quo or deny the importance of providing for peaceful change. Yet no one has better described the core of national self-interest in a stable world order that drives an effective collective-security system.

5

Patterns for a UN Force:
The Five-Power Talks of 1946

The most serious effort to resolve the military problems of an international force took place in 1946 and early 1947, at the hinge between allied wartime cooperation and Cold War competition. For the first and only time, the permanent members of the Security Council held detailed talks on the size, composition, and armed power of a UN force capable of meeting the challenges of the postwar world. Their efforts broke down over differences on the composition and strength of the total force and of their own contributions to it. At the same time, they agreed on equally difficult issues concerning overall control, strategic direction, and command—issues that were central to the effectiveness of a UN force but that had yet to be seriously addressed.

The Key Issues: Force Size and
Permanent-Member Contributions

For fourteen months beginning in February 1946, the permanent members, sitting as the Military Staff Committee (MSC), examined the military implications of Article 43.[1] A major focus of the talks was the size, strength, and composition of the UN force—both from the standpoint of the force as a whole and the individual contributions of the permanent members. All five agreed that the permanent members should, initially at least, provide "the major portion" of the force, an understanding based on a U.S. proposal that the other members had accepted.[2] The delegations differed, however, over the nature of their own contributions and the overall power of the force. On the question of total force size, France, Great Britain, and the Republic of China joined the Soviet Union in opposition to the United States, which advocated an armed force of extraordinary power. The final U.S. estimate of overall force strength, as reported to the Security Council by the Military Staff Committee on April 30, 1947, was two to three times that of the other members. The United States proposed a ground force of twenty divisions (plus required air transport), an air force of 1,250 bombers and 2,250 fighters, and a navy composed of three battleships, six aircraft carriers, fifteen cruisers, eighty-four destroyers, and ninety submarines.[3] Of the other parties, France's estimate was closest to that of the United States, the USSR's was furthest away, and those of Britain and China fell in between.[4]

What potential aggressor did the United States have in mind in proposing a force of such size and power? To many it seemed that the only state that could mount the kind of major aggression that warranted such overwhelming power was the Soviet Union. Certainly the Soviets themselves seem to have regarded the U.S. position as a sign that they were the presumptive adversary. Yet the veto ruled out the use of UN military power against a permanent member, and there is no evidence that the United States had reversed its insistence on permanent-member unanimity. The tendency has been to look for Cold War motivation in the U.S. position. At the least, as Inis Claude suggests, the United States was "curiously unwilling to recognize the fact that the terms of reference of the projected international force excluded the possibility of its being used" against a permanent member because of the veto.[5]

The Cold War explanation is almost certainly a part of the picture.[6] Yet it not only runs into the veto problem but it also cuts across the continuing U.S. objective in 1946 of building cooperative relations among the great powers to make the UN work. The timing of the U.S. decisionmaking process for the MSC talks is important in this regard. The U.S. position was developed in late 1945 and early 1946, at a time when the concert of power on which the UN system rested was still in place, if barely so.[7] The USSR had not yet consolidated its position in Eastern Europe or threatened the territorial integrity of Iran and Greece, and declassified documents show that the United States was reluctant to abandon the security system that had been concluded just six months earlier.

Indeed, the continuing U.S. interest in a functioning UN security system is stated unambiguously in a policy paper of December 28, 1945: "United States policy is to support wholeheartedly the United Nations" and to ensure that the Security Council, "as soon as it comes into existence, [initiates] the formulation of plans for, and the negotiation of . . . an agreement" on the composition of a UN force. Early negotiation of the special agreements is essential, the paper continues, "since their conclusion is prerequisite to the effective functioning of the Security Council."[8]

Formal instructions were transmitted to the U.S. delegation four months later in a document entitled "U.S. Guidance As to the Armed Forces to Be Made Available to the Security Council of the United Nations." The instructions were prepared by the Joint Chiefs of Staff, revised in collaboration with the Department of State, cleared by the State-War-Navy Coordinating Committee, and approved in April 1946 by President Harry S. Truman. The central recommendation calls for a U.S. contribution of "one corps comprising two divisions, a balanced task force of 5 wings, one carrier task group, amphibious and sea transport for the above forces to the extent available, plus adequate surface support."[9] This document, and the memoranda of conversations concerning it, focus mainly on military considerations unrelated to the emerging competition with the Soviet Union.[10]

When congressional leaders were consulted about the proposed U.S. contribution at President Truman's request, they expressed surprise at its size and at the overall dimensions of the UN force that it presupposed. Senator Arthur H. Vandenberg thought that "an aggregate of earmarked forces numbering in the neighborhood of a million from the five permanent members was too large, inasmuch as the forces cannot be used against them but only against other powers."[11] Concerned also about the cost of so large a force and its effect on a war-weary public, Vandenberg would have preferred a U.S. contribution of a single division instead of an entire corps. He was told that the U.S. military "felt that the proposed size of the U.S. land forces contingent could not be reduced below two divisions without raising serious questions as to command. The purpose was to have one corps which would include headquarters troops."[12]

However compelling the questions of command, the huge U.S. contribution that Washington proposed can hardly have been calculated without the assumption of a hypothetical enemy. At the time this could only have been the Soviet Union (the dangers of a partitioned China being three years into the future). Even at this early date, it is possible that the U.S. position on force size may have been based on a scenario of Soviet-inspired aggression like that which in fact occurred five years later in Korea—aggression that required the leadership of a powerful U.S. national force to defeat.

This thinking is implicit in a statement to the Security Council by the British representative, Alexander Cadogan, on June 10, 1947, during the council's consideration of the five powers' report on the MSC talks. Cadogan declared that "if any one of the permanent members, guilty of a breach of the peace or of an act of aggression, were to call a halt to [a UN] force, the remainder of the United Nations would be entitled, under [Article 51], to take action against that Member . . . [using the] forces already made available to the Security Council."[13] If the international force had not already been a dead issue, this statement would have been the last nail in its coffin. But Cadogan's statement was made well into the Cold

War, after Soviet expansionist intentions had become unmistakable through its actions in Iran, Greece, and Eastern Europe.

My own sense is that although the U.S. position on force size may have been reinforced by the growing evidence that East-West cooperation in the UN would be impossible, the U.S. military also wanted to ensure that its forces had the strength to deal with a worst-case threat, including confrontation with the Soviet Union. It may be that domestic pressures for demobilization also led each service branch to press for the largest possible representation in the UN force to protect its own combat effectiveness.

The consultations with congressional leaders on the five-power talks included an interesting exchange on the special regional responsibilities of the permanent members or, more accurately, their spheres of influence. Clearly motivated by Monroe Doctrine considerations, Vandenberg proposed that the MSC report include the following principle: "Armed Forces, in the first instance, so far as practicable, shall be drawn for use from the geographic or regional areas involved." Not surprisingly, he was told that "[U.S.] military authorities . . . feared that specification of the regionalism formula might enable other countries to exclude [U.S. forces] from participation in other regions."[14] Today, as local threats to the peace crowd the agenda of the Security Council, Vandenberg's emphasis on the need for regional powers to bear their share of the burden in the maintenance of regional security has a special resonance.

The approaching Cold War was reflected in other unsettled positions at the talks besides force size and composition. Particularly troublesome to the USSR was the noncommunist members' insistence that the permanent members' military contributions to a UN force be "comparable" in strength and composition but not necessarily "equal." The Western powers argued that the logical path was to make up an international force from the military elements that each member was best equipped to contribute. To the Soviets, "comparability" meant that they would provide most of the ground forces while the other members contributed the projected power of the force through air and naval units.

To some observers at the time, the U.S. position on "comparability" seemed to be an effort to leave the door open for "the United States . . . if required, [to] contribute a nuclear striking force."[15] Although this may have been intended as a future option, declassified documents indicate that the United States did not plan to arm the initial U.S. units with nuclear weapons. In discussions with the State Department, Senator Vandenberg asked "whether the atom bomb was included in the weapons of the proposed U.S. contingent." He was told that it was not.[16]

From the Soviet standpoint, another disquieting position was the opposition of the other four powers to a fixed time limit for the withdrawal of UN troops to their home bases.[17] To set withdrawal in motion, the noncommunist members insisted on a positive decision of the Security Council: that is, a decision in which the veto would apply. This is the same position that the Western powers insisted on forty-five years later in the Persian Gulf war, for much the same reasons.

For the USSR, the threat from these Western positions was increased by the nine-to-two majority that the noncommunist states held on most issues in the Security Council. By 1947 the Soviets had already had some experience with the ways in which the United States and its allies used the council to further their interests at Soviet expense. They had every reason to think that this majority could, and would, be used to control the operations of an international force if one were established. In short, a UN force spelled nothing but trouble for the plans the Soviets had for their neighbors.

Authority and Control, Strategic Direction, and Tactical Command

Although the questions of total force size and permanent-member contributions were the chief obstacles to agreement, they were only two of forty-one issues (or "articles") that the MSC considered. Of these, twenty-five were accepted unanimously, whereas the other sixteen were accompanied by qualifications and exceptions that represented the opposing views of the participants. Because of the general perception that the MSC talks were wholly unproductive, it may be useful to note some of the issues on which the permanent members agreed. The most important points of agreement were:

1. The UN armed forces shall be composed of the best-trained and equipped units of national land, sea, and air forces normally maintained as components of the armed forces of the member nations.
2. The "moral weight and the potential power" behind any decision to employ the forces available to the Security Council will directly influence the size of the forces required. [The intent of this curiously worded article is explained below.]
3. The strength of the UN forces shall be limited to a strength sufficient to enable the Security Council to take prompt action in any part of the world for the maintenance or the restoration of international peace and security.
4. The degree of preparedness of the overall UN force should either be readiness for combat or, at a minimum, the capacity to be brought up to that status in time to execute the primary mission.

5. To facilitate the early establishment of a UN force, the permanent members shall contribute initially the major portion of the armed forces.

6. Member nations unable to furnish armed forces may fulfill their obligation to the UN by furnishing facilities and other assistance.

7. In view of the military advantages that would accrue, the employment of the armed forces should, whenever possible, be initiated in time to forestall, or to suppress promptly, a breach of the peace or an act of aggression. [This is another aspect of the importance to collective security of a rapid-deployment capability.]

8. When engaged in action, the armed forces will be based in areas designated by the Security Council. [One of the most controversial positions, to which the USSR did not agree, was the Western proposal that UN forces, when not in action, should be distributed in bases that were so located geographically as to enable prompt action in any part of the world.]

9. When the UN forces are in action, "they shall come under the control of the Security Council" [the word "control" being translated into French as "autorité"]. [Although accepted by the United States in the MSC negotiations, the phrase "Security Council control" became anathema to Washington two decades later in General Assembly discussions on peacekeeping guidelines, largely because the Soviets used the phrase to diminish the secretary general's responsibilities in the conduct of peacekeeping operations.]

10. The Military Staff Committee shall "be responsible, under the Security Council, for the strategic direction" of the forces while they are in action.

11. An overall commander, or overall commanders, of the armed forces made available to the Security Council may be appointed by the latter, on the advice of the Military Staff Committee, for the duration of the employment of the armed forces by the council. [To this article, France and Britain would have added a sentence leaving open the possibility that the Security Council might appoint separate commanders in chief of land, sea, or air forces, acting under the supreme commander.]

12. The command of national contingents shall be exercised by commanders appointed by the respective contributory nations. These commanders will be entitled to communicate directly with the authorities of their own country on all matters.[18]

Articles nine through twelve—on political control, strategic direction, tactical command, and national-contingent command—derive from a U.S. proposal. That proposal was in turn based on an internal memorandum from the U.S. representatives to the MSC talks setting forth their views concerning the principles on which Article 43 agreements should be based. This memorandum of March 15, 1946, and the policy papers that flowed from it, represent the highest-level government-wide statement of the U.S. position on the management of an international force that has ever been developed. On strategic direction and command, it read: "United Nations forces, when operating under the direction of the Security Council, shall serve under the over-all commander designated by the Security Council. The over-all commander shall act under the strategic direction of the Military Staff Committee."[19]

Implications for an International Deterrent Force

If the permanent members were to hold talks today on the establishment of a UN force, most of the issues that were discussed in 1946—both those that were agreed upon and those that were not—would need to be reexamined in light of present national interests. The first problem that would have to be resolved concerns the criteria for determining force size and power: How does one determine the strength of an international force when it is impossible to know when and where the next threat will come from? It is possible, of course, to work from a worst-case scenario. But is there no way to devise a more helpful principle for calculating the needs of a UN force, one that avoids the political, financial, and preparedness problems of the worst-case hypothesis?

The place to start would seem to be a clear definition of the purpose of a UN force. That must logically be the same as the purpose of the collective security system it serves: the deterrence of aggression and the maintenance of peace. Although it may not seem so at first glance, the deterrence criterion leads to a quite different force structure from that of the worst-case scenario. For one thing, it avoids the problem of the "second strongest adversary," whose military power may call for an entirely different kind of UN force from that needed to defeat enemy number one (if, for example, one is a land power and the other a sea power). It keeps clear of abstract, unproductive debates over the relative merits of different branches of the military services.[20] Finally, the deterrence criterion avoids the fatal flaw of the worst-case principle: branding one state the most likely aggressor by tailoring force composition to that state's military power *before* the Security Council determines that a threat to the peace exists. That path cuts off avenues of conciliation and could precipitate the very aggression that the UN is trying to prevent.

If the primary purpose of the UN system is not to expel aggressors from the territory they have seized—the "peace-through-war" function, as it has been called—but to prevent them from starting wars they cannot win, the size and composition requirements of a UN force change significantly. With the emphasis on deterrence, the function of the force is to convince the would-be aggressor that he will be confronted by a coalition of nations that his military forces cannot hope to defeat. There are a number of ways to make this point clear and credible in a collective-security deterrent system, as mentioned in the summary and elaborated in Chapter 8.

One of the agreed principles in the MSC report that is important from the standpoint of deterrence is that a UN "force will have behind it the whole weight of the available resources of the United Nations."[21] (This principle appears in somewhat altered language as the second article above.) The concept was proposed by the British during consultations in Washington in April 1946. The idea is in a sense self-evident. For the permanent members in particular, the interests that moved them to vote for the establishment of an enforcement action will ordinarily cause them to see it through, so long as popular and parliamentary support continue. It is a point worth remembering in connection with efforts to keep the size of an international deterrent force within reasonable bounds. As the State Department officer who spoke with the British representative put it, "the implication is that although a nation may contribute only a small fraction of its military establishment to the United Nations, there will be behind this fraction the entire logistical organization and resources of that state."[22]

Even allowing for the complications of the Cold War, the MSC negotiations seem to have been on the wrong track in their worst-case approach to force size and strength. Deterrence does not depend only on the combined power of all of the contributions to a standby force. It depends also on the Security Council's ability to launch small actions quickly—actions involving units from the on-call contingents of the concerned powers, which, if attacked, will lead to the use of overwhelming force by those powers and the defeat of the aggressor.

6

Korea and the Limits of Voluntary Enforcement Action

North Korea's invasion of South Korea in the summer of 1950 led to the UN's first experiment with voluntary enforcement action, initially through the Security Council and then, briefly, through the General Assembly. By legitimating the powerful military operation led by the United States and, in the "Uniting for Peace" resolution, creating machinery for avoiding the veto, the Korean action seemed to infuse new purpose into the United Nations—until reality intruded in the form of the Chinese army. Like the Persian Gulf war forty years later, the Korean experience has much to say about the differences between voluntary and mandatory UN operations in terms of their authority, their direction, their composition, and their outcome.

The UN enforcement action in Korea from 1950 to 1953 is not an advertisement for voluntary collective security. As in the Persian Gulf operation forty years later, the UN security system failed in its primary function of deterrence. In both cases a U.S.-led operation turned back a large-scale invasion, and in both cases the aggression would not have occurred if the aggressors had known that they would be opposed by a UN coalition of three nuclear-armed permanent members and more than a dozen middle and smaller powers—and certain, humiliating defeat. Aggression in Korea, as later in the Gulf, was the result of uncertainty about the makeup of the opposition. The point of a collective-security deterrent system is to replace that doubt with certainty.

The members of the UN came to view the Korea action as a bad precedent for other reasons as well. First, the Security Council and the troop contributors lost control of the operation to the United States. Second, the UN umbrella did not greatly enhance the power of the force: The great powers took part because the Soviet- and China-backed aggression threatened their vital interests, and the other contributors were allies of the West. Finally, the UN's military support of one superpower in a conflict that affected the strategic interests of both brought the world to the brink of nuclear war.

Launching a Voluntary Operation

When more than 90,000 North Korean troops crossed the thirty-eighth parallel on the morning of June 25, 1950, the UN response was shaped by two unusual circumstances. First, the secretary general, and through him the Security Council, received exceptionally fast and objective reporting on the invasion from UN representatives who witnessed the attack. (As members of the United Nations Commission on Korea, or UNCOK, these officials had been sent to South Korea to help bring about the unification of the north and south and verify the withdrawal of the occupying forces.) Second, the Soviet Union was absent from the Security Council for the crucial five weeks after the invasion. This enabled the council to adopt three key resolutions. On June 25 it "noted with grave concern the armed attack upon the Republic of Korea by forces from North Korea" and determined under Article 39 that "this action constituted a breach of the peace"; on June 27 it recommended that UN members "furnish such assistance to the Republic of Korea as may be necessary to repel the armed attack"; and on July 7 it recommended that all members providing military units "make such forces . . . available to a unified command under the United States."

The USSR's absence from the Security Council during this turning point of the Cold War is worth a digression. The Soviets maintained that they were boycotting the council to protest the UN's refusal to turn over Nationalist China's seat to Beijing, an explanation that has been widely accepted. The story's credibility rests largely on the fact that the USSR had not participated in the work of the council for a full six months before the invasion.[1] Even if the Soviets were in fact protesting Communist China's exclusion, the question remains why Soviet Ambassador Jacob Malik failed to return to the council directly after the North Korean invasion to veto the early resolutions. Henry Kissinger, for one, argues that Malik would surely have done so "had [he] been less terrified of Stalin or been able to obtain instructions more rapidly."[2]

This explanation is too ingenuous to be believed of the well-oiled Soviet foreign-policy machine. In light of the heavy reliance of North Korean forces on Soviet arms and advisers, there can be no doubt that the USSR had advance knowledge of, and indeed helped to plan, the invasion of South Korea. That being the case, the most disagreeable place for a Soviet representative to be during the invasion would be the Security Council. Even the veto had its disadvantages; its use would underline

Soviet complicity, while the crucial question of U.S. military involvement would probably not depend on Security Council authority.

In later years, the Soviets promoted the notion that they had blundered in absenting themselves from the council at the start of the Korean War—an admission that was itself uncharacteristic of Soviet behavior.[3] The most plausible explanation for the absence of the Soviet delegation—and the only dissenting voice to the Chinese representation explanation that I am aware of—is that of Raymond Aron. "The Soviet delegate," he argues, "intended to return once South Korea had been totally occupied to offer a means of saving face for everyone."[4] Whatever the precise reasons for Soviet nonparticipation, the boycott ended on August 1 when the USSR assumed the rotating Security Council presidency, at which point the council ceased to be an effective organ for the coordination of military support for South Korea.

Even without Soviet participation, the council's establishment of the unified command was a near thing. The authorizing resolution of July 7 received the bare number of seven affirmative votes needed for adoption, with Yugoslavia, India, and Egypt abstaining and the Soviet Union absent. From the sidelines, the Soviets argued that this and the other early resolutions on Korea were invalid because the absence of a permanent member was equivalent to a veto.[5] The majority view, however, was that a member's absence had the same effect as an abstention, which by Security Council precedent did not constitute a negative vote.[6]

The basic distinction between voluntary collective security and the binding system of the charter lies in the council's "recommendations" for military action on June 27 and July 7—as distinct from the "decisions" provided for in Article 42, which require UN members to contribute to enforcement actions if called on by the council to do so. The voluntary nature of the Korean action was not solely the result of the Soviet Union's absence. Even if all of the Security Council members had been present and voting in favor of enforcement action, the council could not have obliged UN members to contribute armed forces because of the absence of Article 43 agreements specifying the nature of each member's contribution.

In this situation, the Security Council went as far as it could in providing political cover for the Korean action. Unlike the voluntary UN action in the Persian Gulf, for example, it authorized the unified command to fly the flag of the United Nations along with the flags of the participating states. The United States was asked to designate the commander of the UN forces, and on July 8 President Truman complied by appointing General Douglas MacArthur commanding general.

Twenty-two of the UN's sixty members offered military contingents, of which sixteen were accepted as being of usable quality and strength. The United States contributed about 50 percent of the ground units, 86 percent of the naval forces, and 93 percent of the air forces, or a total of nearly two-thirds of the UN force. South Korean troops, once fully mobilized and trained, made up much of the remainder, totaling 40 percent of the ground units, 7 percent of the navy, and 6 percent of the air force.

As might be expected, UN members were more willing to furnish humanitarian aid than combat forces, and readier still to support the UN operation in principle. As hundreds of thousands of refugees fled before advancing North Korean forces in the first weeks of battle, thirty governments responded to a Security Council request for relief assistance by contributing such items as medical supplies, field hospitals, food, clothing, and transport facilities. Twenty members, consisting mainly of the Soviet bloc and Arab states (the latter protesting the UN's inaction on the Palestine question), offered no assistance at all. Secretary General Trygve Lie nevertheless reported that fifty-three governments (that is, all nations outside the Soviet bloc) had signified to him their willingness to support the principles contained in the Security Council's resolutions.[7]

Aron argues that the refusal of most members to participate militarily in such a cut-and-dried case of aggression as Korea reveals a basic flaw in the premises of collective security. The gap between the readiness to vote for military sanctions and the unwillingness to take part in them shows, in his view, how unreliable a system is that rests on the willingness of states to fight in wars that do not affect them. "The South American bloc has twenty voices," he writes, "but how many divisions has it offered?" And gathering steam, "it would be absurd to believe that the unfolding of events in Korea has any connection to the grandiose proposals of the representatives of thirty or forty countries, who are firmly resolved to speak and vote as they please but not to take part in military operations."[8]

This passage appeared in *Le Figaro* on February 1, 1951, after Communist China's intervention had created a new war and UN forces seemed about to be driven from the Korean peninsula. Aron is reflecting a growing concern about the wisdom of baptizing as collective security an operation whose control lies in the hands of one power. This was a marked change from the earlier enthusiasm that most Westerners felt for this novel type of voluntary UN action that seemed capable of circumventing the veto. Although tied to military setbacks that were later reversed, the new skepticism about ad hoc collective security left a legacy that lasted through the Cold War.

The Rise and Fall of General Assembly Support

If February 1951 was a low point in the confidence of UN members in an operation that had passed largely beyond their control, the high point occurred three months earlier with the General Assembly's adoption of the resolution known as "Uniting for Peace."[9] Proposed by the United States and supported by Great Britain and France, the resolution authorizes the General Assembly to recommend enforcement measures if the Security Council cannot act due to lack of unanimity among the permanent members. It provides the machinery for such action by authorizing special sessions of the assembly if requested by a majority of UN members or any seven members of the council. Finally, it recommends two useful measures that have been generally ignored. The first is that every member "maintain within its armed forces elements so trained, organized, and equipped that they could promptly be made available" to either the council or the assembly; the second suggests that a Peace Observation Commission be set up "to observe and report on the situation in any area where there exists international tension."

The General Assembly, Senator Arthur H. Vandenberg's "town meeting of the world," soon proved incapable not only of running a military action but of legitimating it. After the intervention of China, the General Assembly served mainly as a forum for trying to prevent the eruption of a full-scale war among the great powers. Proposals for a compromise settlement proliferated, launched primarily by India and other Asian and African states but drawing considerable support from Western members.[10] The misgivings of the members at large, combined with the special concerns of the troop contributors, created a climate of extreme caution toward any measures that risked further escalation. This was reflected in a reluctance to impose serious economic sanctions on China. After a five-month effort by the United States, the assembly finally called for an embargo on the shipment of strategic items to China in May 1951. The sanctions had little impact, however, since each member was allowed to "determine which commodities . . . fall within the embargo."[11]

More damaging than the General Assembly initiatives was the shrinking confidence in the military strategy and political judgment of the United States. The reason for this new atmosphere was the U.S. decision to pursue the remnants of the North Korean army to the Yalu River boundary with China—an event that precipitated China's entry into the war and led to "the greatest defeat suffered by American arms since the Battle of Manassas and an international disaster of the first water."[12] For most UN members, it mattered little whether the decision to drive to the Chinese border was made by the U.S. government or by a commanding general whom the government could not control.

Having authorized limited UN operations in North Korea, the General Assembly bears some responsibility for the chain of events that led to China's intervention. The authority to operate north of the thirty-eighth parallel was contained in General Assembly Resolution 376(V) of October 7, 1950, which recommended that "all appropriate steps be taken to ensure conditions of stability throughout Korea." The intention was to permit UN forces to prepare the way in North Korea for UN supervision of elections for an independent, democratic, and united Korea. It was clear from the debate, however, that although there was support for limited action north of the parallel, "there was equally strong insistence that all reasonable steps should be taken to avoid provoking the intervention of Communist China or the Soviet Union."[13]

The situation in the General Assembly was complicated by the lack of information about U.S. strategy. It was not until late November 1950, when UN forces were in full retreat, that the State Department began holding weekly briefings on military and political developments for the representatives of the troop-contributing governments. This forum, known as the Committee of Sixteen, was the closest thing to a consultative institution that the UN operation produced. More sensitive information was transmitted to close allies through intelligence channels and bilateral discussions; yet it appears that the only instance in which U.S. strategy changed as a result of such discussions was the cancellation of plans for the "hot pursuit" of enemy aircraft across the Yalu River.[14] In contrast to the Gulf war, consultations among the troop contributors were rarely held at the head-of-government level. The conspicuous exception was British Prime Minister Clement Attlee's hasty visit to Washington in November 1950 after President Truman gave the impression at a press briefing that he was considering the use of atomic weapons against China.

The brief experiment with "Uniting for Peace" demonstrated the obvious: that the General Assembly is not a viable forum for directing an enforcement action. In the immediate aftermath of an armed attack, a majority of the membership may agree that the UN should take action to restore the peace. That consensus is subject to great strain, however, as soon as the hard decisions have to be made on the conduct of the operation, its precise objectives, and the conditions of its termination.

Numbers, Effectiveness, and Size of National Contingents

If the General Assembly's authority to undertake enforcement action is no longer a live issue in the post–Cold War era, debate nevertheless continues over the relative merits of voluntary versus binding action by the Security Council. One aspect of this debate concerns the quantity and quality of the contingents needed for effective military action and equitable burden sharing. On this the Korean War is instructive.

There is no doubt that the United States bore a disproportionate share of the military burden in Korea. And there is no question that the assumption of that burden served important U.S. interests. The leadership role in Korea was a clear signal that direct or indirect aggression against U.S. interests would be opposed with the force necessary to defeat it. U.S. allies received the assurance they needed that Washington could be counted on to defend them in Cold War confrontations. Why then did so many noncommunist countries that supported the UN action decline to take part in it? And what would have been the consequences if they had participated?

The first step is to take a closer look at the composition of the UN force. Of the sixteen members whose contingents were accepted for action, three were permanent members (the United States, France, and Great Britain), six were middle powers (Australia, Belgium, Canada, the Netherlands, Greece, and Turkey), and seven were smaller powers (Colombia, Ethiopia, Luxembourg, New Zealand, the Philippines, Thailand, and the Union of South Africa). Most of the eight contingents that were not accepted were turned down because they were too small, the U.S. military having decided that the minimum size for effective action was a reinforced battalion. Political considerations also entered the selection process, as they have in virtually all UN peacekeeping and enforcement operations. The most important exclusion was Nationalist China, which offered a substantial force but was rejected in order to avoid provoking the intervention of Communist China.

In addition to the sixteen troop contributors, Japan also played a part in the defeat of North Korea. Its most important contribution was to provide the staging area from which the U.S. amphibious assault at Inchon was launched on September 15, 1950. This brilliant operation, designed by MacArthur, led to the recapture of Seoul and the near-total destruction of the 400,000-man North Korean army. The UN Charter anticipates regional-power help like Japan's by specifying that UN members may furnish "assistance and facilities" in lieu of armed forces in fulfillment of their Article 43 obligations. In later years, Japan was to provide a rapid-deployment capability in peacekeeping missions by airlifting UN contingents from their home countries to their areas of operation.

Useful as this nonmilitary assistance is, it is a different order of sacrifice from the human costs of combat. The problem for Japan and Germany is that their post–World War II constitutions prohibit the dispatch of forces abroad, even for peacekeeping missions with defensive mandates. There are signs of a desire for change in both countries; indeed, in Bosnia, Germany took its first steps toward participation in UN peacekeeping missions that directly affect its security. For both governments, the issue is tied to permanent membership in the Security Council. In March 1997 the first steps in that direction took place, as UN members began to discuss concrete proposals for the permanent participation of Japan, Germany, and a number of major Asian and African states. This kind of enlargement is overdue: Adjusting the permanent membership (but not the veto power) of the Security Council to reflect contemporary power realities would enhance the legitimacy and authority of the council.

Korea was the first test of the members' willingness to participate in a UN enforcement action in the absence of Article 43 agreements. Some states did cite this as a reason for not participating. Their argument was that their "enabling legislation assumed the existence of special agreements under Article 43 and consequently did not come into operation in the absence of such agreements."[15] But the absence of the smaller powers did not make a big difference. What counted militarily was that four out of the five permanent members either contributed troops or offered them; the principal regional power and the nation attacked made major contributions; and most of the other participating states provided well-trained and armed contingents. Although the participation of UN members was far from ideal from the standpoint of burden sharing, the ingredients for the efficient use of collective force were present.

Problems in the Termination of an
Ad Hoc Operation

In Korea, as later in the Persian Gulf, some of the most controversial decisions concerned the forward limits of a UN force in hot pursuit of the enemy. It is impossible to know whether a charter-based UN action would have reached the same decisions as the ad hoc operation did in Korea, but the question is worth considering.

The United States made all of the central decisions on the time and place for terminating the Korean operation. First, it decided to accept the status quo ante, Secretary Acheson stating in July 1950 that U.S. action in response to the Security Council's resolutions was "solely for the purpose of restoring the Republic of Korea to its status prior to the invasion from the north."[16] Next, as General MacArthur's forces approached the thirty-eighth parallel, it made the decision to conduct "properly restricted" operations in North Korea in order "to destroy the invader's force" and pave the way for unification of the north and south.[17] Then it decided to acquiesce in MacArthur's disregard of those restrictions, leading to the UN's advance to the Yalu River, China's entry into the war, and the subsequent retreat of UN forces to positions south of Seoul.

In April 1951, the tide of battle having turned once more, Washington decided to leave the unification of Korea to later negotiations and to seek a cease-fire along a defensible line north of the thirty-eighth parallel.[18] China accepted the U.S. cease-fire proposal, but, apparently because of miscommunication in its transmission, understood that the peace talks were to be based on a demarcation line along the thirty-eighth parallel rather than the line of battle and refused to abandon the North Korean territory held by the UN.[19] At this turn of events, the Truman administration decided to continue the fighting, resulting in nearly as many U.S. casualties over the next two years as in the first year of the war—a total of about 142,000 Americans killed, wounded, and missing, not to speak of the casualties of the other UN contributors. On July 27, 1953, with a new administration in office, the United States decided to end the hostilities on a line that snakes from southwest to northeast of the thirty-eighth parallel.

Despite heavy losses, the contributing states stood fast and cooperated fully with the U.S. command throughout the war. General MacArthur said of these forces that "the United Nations, the various nations who have contributed there, the troops, the actual commands there, have been splendid in every respect."[20] The U.S. military, for its part, showed itself adept at running a complex multinational operation with order and efficiency, as it did forty years later in the Persian Gulf. This was despite the command-and-control problems that inevitably arise in ad hoc operations where there has been no opportunity for the joint planning and training needed for large-scale collective actions.

Some of the difficulties that a democracy encounters in terminating a war at the right time and place have been discussed in Chapter 4. Others were tragically demonstrated in Vietnam. Korea carries its own lessons, although important elements of the situation were unique. Certainly no commanding general is likely to reappear with the extraordinary military reputation, open disdain for government policy, and special appeal to the far Right as General MacArthur.[21] And the Cold War power configuration will not repeat itself, although one would have thought that the risk of nuclear conflict in Korea would have reinforced the importance of halting the war at the place where it began.

There seem to have been two main reasons for the U.S. decision to continue the war beyond the thirty-eighth parallel. First was the displacement of political objectives by military goals. In part this resulted from the apparent possibility of achieving more than the original UN goals after the rout of the North Korean army in the fall of 1950. Reinforcing this was the U.S. tradition of deference to a field commander's judgments on strategy and tactics, going back at least as far as Abraham Lincoln's unwillingness to interfere with the decisions of his generals. The second reason stemmed from domestic politics. The Truman administration was vulnerable to right-wing attacks because of its earlier resistance to pressure to roll back communism in Asia, making it difficult to remove MacArthur when he first disregarded the restrictions on his forward movement in October 1950.

From the standpoint of the direction and control of UN enforcement actions, Korea has other lessons. The war showed that the efficient use of collective force requires that consistent, consensus-based policy guidance be provided to the commander reflecting not only the original purposes of an operation but its evolving goals as the situation unfolds. It showed that in voluntary no less than binding actions, policy direction that flows from a UN mandate can have a steadying effect on domestic pressures. Finally, it showed that key strategic decisions, like the timing of cease-fire overtures, require consultations with the troop-contributing states and the Security Council. Without such consultations, the operation is likely to lose the domestic and international support that was the reason for seeking UN authority in the first place.

7

Peacekeeping and Peaceful Settlement: Namibia and the Arab-Israeli Dispute

In the thirty-five years that followed the UN enforcement action in Korea, the Security Council explored the peaceful end of the conciliation-coercion spectrum and found a number of ways to combine peacekeeping with peaceful-settlement activity. Almost all of these Cold War peacekeeping missions were consensual. Dispatched normally after a cease-fire with the agreement of the parties that had been at war, they were governed by rules of engagement that restricted the use of force to self-defense. In the two instances in which UN peacekeeping missions were launched without the agreement of all of the key players (the Congo in 1960 and Lebanon in 1978), the results were less than wholly successful.[1]

The purpose of most of these Cold War missions was to defuse conflicts in strategically important regions so as to lessen their ability to draw the nuclear powers into direct confrontation. UN Secretary General Dag Hammarskjöld provided the conceptual basis for this goal in his theory of "preventive diplomacy," which aimed to prevent Third World disputes from becoming a part of the East-West conflict.[2] There was also an element of nation building in Hammarskjöld's thinking. By helping to maintain security and establish democratic institutions, Hammarskjöld believed that the UN could help nations emerging from colonialism take their first steps free from outside interference.

In the last few years of the Cold War before Mikhail Gorbachev came to power in 1985, most UN peacekeeping and peaceful-settlement activities were on hold.[3] No new peacekeeping missions had been launched since the 1978 operation in Lebanon (UNIFIL). In Cyprus, Afghanistan, Cambodia, Namibia, the Falklands, and the Iran-Iraq conflict, UN mediation efforts were marking time. The reasons are clear. Most of the serious disputes of the early 1980s were either theaters of East-West rivalry or regional quarrels whose peaceful settlement was not vital to great-power interests. In addition, the posturing of nonaligned/Soviet bloc majorities in the General Assembly and the anti-UN reaction in the United States spilled over into peacekeeping and peacemaking. It was in 1985 that large U.S. withholdings began, not only of assessed U.S. contributions but also of payments to peacekeeping operations that Washington had supported and, in the case of UNIFIL, taken the initiative in establishing.

The early post–Cold War period, especially the years from 1988 to 1993, which are the focus of this chapter, were marked by new combinations of consensual and nonconsensual force. These ranged from nation building in Namibia, where a Security Council agreement had to be carried out with an unanticipated degree of force, to the tripwire force along the Iraq-Kuwait border, which combined collective security and peacekeeping, and finally to the two "peace enforcement" missions in Somalia, which are treated in Chapter 9.

Changing Patterns of Regional Conflict After the Cold War

Two kinds of regional conflict have dominated the post–Cold War years, each with different implications for the UN's peace-and-security functions. First is the dispute that threatens the important interests of a major military state. Often involving the expansion of a dominant regional power, the challenge may be to the economic, political, or strategic interests of the major power. The regional state that is threatened is likely to have ties to one or more permanent members of the Security Council. The classic case, of course, is the 1991 war in the Persian Gulf. This confrontation met all the conditions for permanent-member involvement and added, for good measure, the elements of clear-cut aggression and incipient nuclear-weapons capabilities.

The second category of regional conflict involves smaller countries in areas of secondary strategic importance over issues that primarily concern the disputants. This low-level violence can have a number of causes. Ethnic minorities seek autonomy, supported by states that share their culture and opposed by others that fear the spread of separatism within their own borders. Population growth begins to outstrip the ability of the poorer states to feed their own people, creating pressures to seize the territory of others. Religious fundamentalism joins secular fanaticism in attacking Western interests as the economic gap widens between North and South. And throughout this mingling of ethnic, religious, political, and economic antagonisms, longtime rivals arm themselves with weapons of increasingly destructive capability.

These local disputes raise some of the hardest questions for UN peace-keeping and enforcement action. Do conflicts of this kind really threaten "international peace and security" in the meaning intended by the UN Charter? What interests do the permanent members and others not directly involved have in contributing forces to keep the peace in such areas? If there is such interest, how can the burden be fairly shared between the regional states with the greatest stake in the settlement and the permanent members who alone may have the power to suppress the aggression? These questions will be addressed in this and the next two chapters. One of the safer predictions is that the transition from one international order to another will continue to be turbulent; and in this climate, some of the hardest decisions will concern conflicts that have little to do with the strategic interests of the major powers.

Nation Building Since the Cold War: The Case of Namibia

Namibia is the first and most successful example of the Security Council's effectiveness in dispute settlement during the years of permanent-member cooperation that peaked about two years after Mikhail Gorbachev's rise to power in 1985. In Namibia, the result of the new power configuration was Security Council agreement on a broad UN mandate to oversee the withdrawal of outside forces and monitor the transition to democracy. U.S.-Soviet cooperation sheltered the negotiations from extremists on both sides, undercutting both the right-wing elements in South Africa and the most militant left-wing groups in the African states and national liberation movements.

The question of Namibia engaged the United Nations throughout the decolonization process, serving mainly as a subject for polemics in debates on North-South and East-West issues. UN actions during the Cold War were considered suspect by Africans on both sides of the dispute. South Africa looked at the hostile majority in the General Assembly and concluded that the UN was incapable of acting impartially. The "front-line states" of southern Africa and the South West Africa People's Organization (SWAPO) were equally disillusioned. After a succession of Western vetoes of proposed sanctions against South Africa, they had concluded by the mid–1970s that the path to Namibian independence lay through force rather than negotiations.

In 1977 the administration of President Jimmy Carter launched the most serious effort of the Cold War to untie this last tangled knot of colonialism. The five Western members of the Security Council, working as a "contact group," opened a dialogue between South Africa and SWAPO and managed to secure agreement on the principles for a final settlement.

In 1978 these principles were embodied in Security Council Resolution 435. As part of an elaborate transition process to Namibian independence, Resolution 435 called for national elections administered by South Africa but supervised by the United Nations. At the same time, at the Security Council's request, the secretary general submitted a proposal for the supervision of elections by a United Nations Transition Assistance Group (UNTAG) made up of military, civilian, and police components. Despite protracted delays because of South Africa's objections to UN ideas for implementing the principles of the settlement and because of a growing Cuban military presence in Angola, Resolution 435 remained for the next ten years the definitive plan for Namibian self-determination.

The Effects of Soviet Cooperation

The final breakthrough in southern Africa occurred eight years into the Ronald Reagan administration, which had consistently linked the withdrawal of South African forces from Namibia to the pullback of Cuba's 20,000–25,000 troops from Angola. On August 8, 1988, under U.S. mediation, Angola, Cuba, and South Africa signed a protocol specifying the sequence of steps in which South African and Cuban forces would be withdrawn from Namibia and Angola. Although not a party to the protocol, SWAPO told the secretary general that it would honor the cease-fire. One part of the equation that led to agreement was the tenacious mediation of Assistant Secretary of State Chester A. Crocker. Another was Soviet association with the settlement process and the restrictions on the use of force that flowed from it. As UN Under Secretary General Brian Urquhart wrote at the time, it was "in southern Africa that the new Soviet policy of cooperation within the United Nations for the resolution of regional conflicts [bore] its first fruits."[4]

What, exactly, did the Soviets do to advance the mediation process? In many respects their old Cold War positions did not change. They proposed no changes to the settlement framework, they apparently did not press their Marxist allies to accept specific negotiating positions, and they distanced themselves from the U.S. concept of "linkage" between Namibian independence and Cuban withdrawal until it became clear that the concept would prevail.[5] On the other hand, their declared support for the settlement process strengthened the U.S. hand with each of the parties in 1988 and smoothed the way to agreement in the Security Council. Once the tripartite accord came into effect, the Soviets became part of the quiet diplomatic effort to ensure that it was carried out. In April 1989, for example, after SWAPO had challenged the United Nations by infiltrating its fighters into Namibia, the Soviets worked with the United States to contain the crisis through a joint commission on southern Africa consisting of Angolan, Cuban, and South African officials and U.S. and Soviet observers.[6]

If Soviet policy was driven by the need to end its ruinous military competition with the United States, Washington's South Africa policy was also influenced by global power considerations. One reason for U.S. insistence on the Security Council's endorsement of the Namibia and Angola agreements was that this endorsement represented "an implicit gesture to the Soviets as a permanent member of the Security Council."[7] Indeed, Washington drew the council into the diplomatic process whenever possible. "At every step along the road to settlement," Crocker recalls, "we considered ways to place our diplomacy under a UN umbrella. . . . The decision in 1981 to operate within a UN framework and to retain Resolution 435 as the basis and pivot for a settlement provided indispensable credibility."[8]

In this opening chapter of the post–Cold War era, Soviet diplomats seem to have been trying to carry out Gorbachev's call for superpower cooperation in the resolution of regional conflicts—without, perhaps, being exactly sure how to go about it.[9] They were at least clear that Namibia was the place to start. According to Anatoliy Adamishin, the senior Soviet official for African affairs in 1988, "the prospects for U.S.-Soviet cooperation were better in Southern Africa than in any of the other regional conflicts (i.e., Nicaragua, Afghanistan, Kampuchea)."[10]

The relative passivity of Soviet diplomacy did not lessen the impact of the new superpower relationship on the parties. By 1988 it had become clear to them all that they had exhausted their military options. Angola recognized that the Cuban troops on its soil could not survive a thaw in the Cold War and that it had better take advantage of the negotiating leverage they provided while it could. The frontline states concluded that UN-supervised elections were more likely to ensure SWAPO's accession to power than continued armed struggle. SWAPO itself, though far from enthusiastic about a settlement that provided for continuing aid to Angola while denying it to SWAPO guerrillas, realized that it could not for long sustain its operations without the aid of its supporters. Finally, South Africa saw the increasing weakness of Soviet-backed Marxist regimes and, along with it, the loss of the external threat that had been used to justify its militancy toward its African neighbors.

North-South Differences over UNTAG's Size and Cost

If Security Council endorsement of the Namibia agreements provided legitimacy for the settlement, it was the UN forces on the ground that had to ensure the freedom of the elections, which were the last step on the road to independence. As it turned out, differences over the size and cost of the UN operation were nearly as divisive as intra-African politics. In early 1989 these differences came to a head as the permanent members, led by the United States, insisted that UNTAG's military arm be reduced to 4,650 troops from the 7,500-man force originally envisaged in order to reduce its cost. African members of the council sought to block the reduction, arguing that the smaller force would be unable to prevent South Africa from exercising undue influence over the election process.

The issue surfaced again when the General Assembly considered the financing of the operation, causing a delay in deployment that turned out to have serious consequences. On March 31, 1989, the eve of the date on which outside forces were to begin their withdrawal, the UN had only about 300 soldiers in northern Namibia. On that day SWAPO sent some 2,000 fighters into Namibia from Angola in an attempt to establish UN-recognized bases in anticipation of the coming elections. Since UNTAG was unprepared to repel the attack, Secretary General Javier Pérez de Cuéllar permitted South Africa to do so. SWAPO lost several hundred men in the fighting that followed. Pérez de Cuéllar's action was highly unpopular with the nonaligned group, which issued a communiqué terming his decision an act of "genocide" and declaring its members ashamed to belong to the United Nations.

Especially galling to Third World countries was China's support of the four other permanent members after years in which it had generally followed the Afro-Asian lead. The new possibilities for serious work in the council had evidently given China second thoughts about its carefully cultivated image as a developing country rather than a great power. SWAPO Foreign Secretary Theo Ben Gurirab complained at the time that the new cohesiveness of the superpowers at the UN had turned "the smaller peoples into chips on the chessboard."[11]

After decades of decrying Security Council paralysis, the smaller countries had come full circle to the fears of their forerunners at San Francisco that the permanent members would use the UN to impose settlements on the weak. Security Council recommendations can in fact look much like demands. In the case of Namibia, the political terms of the settlement were tied to the strength of the UN force needed to carry them out. In the end, the African countries had the choice of taking the package plan for Namibian independence or leaving it.

Tensions between the major powers that pay the bills and the smaller countries that need the troops are likely to remain a part of the scene. The interests of the large and small powers may also differ in the formulation of peacekeeping mandates, in the level of permissible force, and in the conditions for mission termination. Indeed, in the Persian Gulf crisis two years later, the same kinds of North-South differences arose. There, the dominant U.S. role heightened sensitivities about great-power manipulation, leading smaller states to say that their cooperation in future UN operations would depend on a greater voice in the decisionmaking process.

From the standpoint of U.S. policy, the case of Namibia showed how easily U.S. political and financial interests can pull in different directions at the UN. For example, the U.S. negotiation of the Namibia agreement—with its important implications for an overall settlement in southern Africa—was jeopardized by U.S. efforts to reduce the cost of carrying out the settlement process. (As it turned out, the cost of the operation was $365 million, making UNTAG the only UN peacekeeping operation to end in a surplus.) In Rwanda five years later, some 500,000 people were massacred as Washington bargained for a higher price for the armored personnel carriers that were needed to move the peacekeeping force, which the United States had just voted to authorize.

Armed Force in the Service of Nation Building

With its dovetailed military, civilian, and police functions, UNTAG was the largest and, administratively, the most complex of the fourteen peace-keeping operations authorized by the Security Council up to that time. (The only similar nation-building enterprise during the Cold War was the UN Temporary Executive Authority [UNTEA], which operated as an international regime in West New Guinea from 1962 to 1963 as the terri-tory was being transferred from the Netherlands to Indonesia.)[12] As it turned out, UNTAG was the forerunner of even more intricate missions, the most ambitious of all being the rebuilding of the Cambodian nation after civil violence had torn it apart. The general trend in peacekeeping has been away from straightforward tasks, like the separation of forces after a cease-fire and the observation of limited-arms zones, and toward the more complicated task of shepherding transitions from authoritarian rule to democracy.

Some sense of the complexity of the Namibia mission can be gathered from a glance at the principal functions of UNTAG's military component. (Although the armed forces made up slightly more than half of the total personnel of 8,000, they accounted for 75 percent of the cost.) The princi-pal military tasks of the peacekeeping force were to:

1. Monitor the cease-fire.
2. Monitor the restriction of South African troops to their bases and their subsequent reduction to the agreed level of 1,500 service personnel.
3. Monitor South African military personnel who continued to perform civilian functions during the transition.

4. Monitor the dismantling of the command structures of the
    various local forces.
5. Monitor the restriction of SWAPO troops to their bases in Angola
    and Zambia. (The principal responsibility for monitoring
    SWAPO fighters lay with the United Nations Angola Verification
    Mission [UNAVEM]; however, with only some seventy military
    observers, UNAVEM was in no position to do its job
    effectively.)[13]

UNTAG's functions are at the high end of any measure of the degree of
difficulty of peacekeeping missions. One of the most thoughtful recent
studies of peacekeeping sets an "ascending order of complexity and in-
trusiveness" of UN operations.[14] At the top of the scale are almost the precise tasks that UNTAG performed—the verification of agreed force with-
drawals, the supervision of the demobilization of local forces, the
maintenance of security conditions necessary for free elections, and, on
the civilian side, the temporary administration of new states.

SWAPO's military challenge to the UN, and to the tripartite agreement
that the Security Council had endorsed, was by far the most difficult
problem on the road to settlement. In addition to the efforts of the concerned powers working through the joint commission, British Prime
Minister Margaret Thatcher and UN Special Representative Martti Ahti-
saari played central roles in resolving the crisis. Even with the help of this
diplomacy, the timetable for elections was set back six weeks by the battle. In retrospect, the UN decision to allow South Africa to use specified
units to drive out the SWAPO fighters is hard to fault. Pérez de Cuéllar
was faced with the Hobson's choice of antagonizing the UN majority or
of presiding over the collapse of the tripartite accord through full-scale
fighting between South Africa and SWAPO and, possibly, repudiation of
the entire agreement by South Africa.

It has been suggested that UNTAG would not have challenged SWAPO
even if all of its military contingents had been deployed: "It is not clear that
[fully deployed UN forces] would have been willing or able to accost
SWAPO, let alone throw themselves between SWAPO's fighters and South
African guns."[15] This misses the point of UN peacekeeping. The UN troops
in Namibia included detachments from some of SWAPO's main supporters: Kenya, Malaysia, and Finland provided the three enlarged infantry
battalions, while a large number of African and nonaligned states were
among the smaller military contributors. It is unlikely that SWAPO would
have attacked these forces if the UN troops and mobile observer units had
been stationed along the length of the border. Furthermore, although
UNTAG had the defensive mandate typical of peacekeeping actions, its
forces were authorized and expected to defend themselves if attacked.

In any peacekeeping operation, the primary deterrent is the inclusion of forces from states that the warring parties are unwilling to confront. The same is true of UN enforcement actions. The chief difference is that Chapter VII actions must also include military powers that, if challenged, can be expected to respond with a level of force that is unacceptable to the aggressor. It is true that the situation in Namibia had unusual elements. The northern border was long and hard to monitor even under the 7,500-man operation originally envisaged. And complicating matters was the fact that the main objective of the UNTAG operation was to protect against South Africa, not SWAPO, resulting in fewer UN troops in the north than would otherwise have been the case. The last thing anyone expected was that SWAPO (presumably with the foreknowledge of Angola) would challenge the agreement it had just accepted.

The Making of a Democratic State

On November 11, 1989, in an electoral process that the UN certified as "free and fair at every stage," more than 97 percent of Namibia's voters turned out to elect a constituent assembly.[16] The lack of intimidation and the calm atmosphere in which the elections took place were due in large measure to the professionalism and teamwork of UNTAG's military and civilian components. One of the foremost experts on UN peacekeeping attributes the success of the Namibia operation not only to the end of superpower rivalry but also to the markedly improved performance of the peacekeepers themselves.[17]

To no one's surprise, SWAPO won an absolute majority in the constituent assembly. But with 57 percent of the votes and forty-one of the seventy-two seats, it did not have the two-thirds majority that would have enabled it to disregard the views of the minority parties. In any case, it soon became clear that SWAPO did not intend to dictate the terms of the constitution but was bent on reconciliation with all Namibians, including white conservatives. By the time Namibia became independent on March 21, 1990, the assembly had agreed on a strikingly democratic constitution based on principles proposed by the United States in 1982.

In the years since independence, Namibia has had more than its share of problems, including a serious fiscal crisis, uneven economic development, and inadequate social services for the black community.[18] At the same time, a multiparty system flourishes, and the 90,000 whites who make up about 5 percent of the population have had little difficulty adjusting to the black leadership that they fought for so long to prevent.[19] SWAPO's respect for the rights of the white citizens of Namibia provided a model for peaceful change that contributed to the seminal changes that followed in South Africa.

Other Uses of Force in the Post–Cold War Era

From Peacekeeping to Nation Building

Namibia is only one of several UN ventures since the end of the Cold War to combine peacemaking and armed force in the service of war prevention and nation building. In Afghanistan and El Salvador, along the Iran-Iraq border and in the Western Sahara, the Security Council intervened in ways that joined classic mediation techniques with a military presence that helped provide a stable climate for negotiation. In addition, an assortment of long-established UN forces, observers, and peacemaking representatives remain in the Middle East, Africa, Cyprus, and the Indian subcontinent.

The founders of the UN believed that peaceful-settlement activity under Chapter VI and enforcement action under Chapter VII were mutually reinforcing, and so they have turned out to be. The effective use of armed force, when it is needed, is tied to the ability of preventive diplomacy to resolve most disputes without the use of force. The interrelationship between armed power and diplomacy was a central part of early collective-security theory. Lord Robert Cecil, with Woodrow Wilson the co-father of collective security, argued that the system depended for its workability on the early, aggressive use of conciliation procedures. He regarded enforcement action as feasible—and hence credible—only if hardly ever used.

In the early 1990s, armed force came to be employed in increasingly intrusive ways. UN troops disarmed insurgents in Nicaragua and Honduras, verified the cessation of aid to rebel movements in other Central American countries, and facilitated the withdrawal of Cuban troops from Angola. Other missions sought to restructure armies and demobilize combatants. In Cambodia the most complex UN peacekeeping operation ever launched was sent to end the violence and organize an interim administration. These are the second-generation peacekeeping missions, which bloomed mainly between 1990 and 1993.[20] Beginning with the Namibia settlement and ending with Somalia, they involved the UN in the domestic affairs of states far more than any of the Cold-War peacekeeping operations except for that in the Congo.

In 1993, second-generation peacekeeping came to an end after the two UN "peace-enforcement" missions in Somalia were drawn into the Somali civil war. At the turn of the century, UN peacekeeping is less ambitious, less intrusive, and less publicized, but no less useful for that.[21] It is characterized by low-risk enterprises where functioning governments ask for help in the transition to democracy. These third-generation operations are typified by cooperative peacekeeping efforts that France, Britain, and the United States have undertaken in Africa.

One example of this collaboration is the election-monitoring operation in the Central African Republic that the Security Council authorized in Resolution 1159 of March 27, 1998. Known as the UN Mission in the Central African Republic (or MINURCA, its French acronym), the mission was created "to provide advice and technical support to the national electoral bodies . . . [for] legislative elections scheduled for August/September 1998." As part of its mandate, MINURCA was directed to assist national security forces in maintaining order and in protecting key installations in the capital. It was also asked to "supervise . . . the final disposition of all weapons retrieved in the course of the disarmament exercise." Unsaid in the resolution is that the disarmament in question had already been carried out by French troops in an earlier unilateral operation. Had that not been the case, the United States would almost certainly have refrained from taking part in MINURCA in light of the bitter controversy over disarmament in Somalia.

The First Tripwire Operations: Iraq-Kuwait and Macedonia

In April 1991 a new kind of UN operation was launched that further obscures the boundary between peacekeeping and collective security—or, put another way, that illustrates the wide range of options available to the Security Council along the conciliation-coercion spectrum. Along the Iraq-Kuwait border and in Macedonia, "tripwire" arrangements that include some or all of the permanent members have proved a useful tool in conflict prevention. Their effectiveness lies in the unspoken but highly credible threat of the major powers to use force to prevent aggression in an area of strategic importance.

Soon after the withdrawal of Iraq's forces from Kuwait, the Security Council established an unarmed observation mission, known as the UN Iraq-Kuwait Observer Mission (or UNIKOM), to monitor the demilitarized zone between Iraq and Kuwait. UNIKOM was to observe any hostile action by one state against the other and to deter violations of the boundary. In February 1993, after a series of incidents along the border, the council increased the strength of the mission and extended its mandate to include the capacity to take military action to prevent violations of the demilitarized zone. To carry out the expanded mandate, the three hundred military observers who made up the original mission were augmented by more than nine hundred troops and military support personnel. Over thirty-three states have contributed troops and observers. But the importance of UNIKOM for the future is that it is the first UN operation to include personnel from all five permanent members.

Although it resembles in its declared functions some of the Middle East missions that separated hostile parties after the Arab-Israeli wars, UNIKOM is radically different. As part of the series of mandatory decisions taken under Chapter VII during the Gulf crisis, the force does not require Baghdad's continuing assent to remain on Iraqi soil—a defining characteristic of the earlier, consensual peacekeeping operations. In purpose and intent, UNIKOM is closer to collective security than to peacekeeping, although it combines elements of both. The participation of all five permanent members makes it plain that renewed Iraqi aggression would lead to a request for further Security Council authority for the use of armed force.

The other ongoing tripwire operation is the UN Preventive Deployment Force (UNPREDEP) in the former Yugoslav republic of Macedonia. Here, four of the permanent members (China does not take part) contribute forces to an operation that is designed to prevent hostilities in the two-year-old crisis between Greece and the former Republic of Macedonia.[22] Established in March 1995 to replace the larger UN Protection Force in Macedonia (UNPROFOR), the present operation has the mild-sounding task of monitoring and reporting border developments that could undermine confidence and stability. But the participation of four permanent members and the deployment of 1,050 troops and 35 observers along the border send the message that military action involving Macedonia would be met with armed force. The U.S. contribution of 550 troops represents the most significant U.S. venture into preventive diplomacy backed by tripwire peacekeeping—other than UNIKOM, which stemmed directly from the Chapter VII enforcement action in the Gulf.

The balance of combat troops versus observers in Iraq and Macedonia is significant. The experience of the first two years of UNIKOM was that unarmed observers could be bypassed or infiltrated by armed irregulars from Iraq without fear of consequences. Troops that can fire at forces violating the demilitarized zone, as is now the case in UNIKOM, are a different matter. Used cautiously, tripwire forces can be an effective way of deterring middle powers that have designs on their smaller neighbors.

The United Nations and the Arab-Israeli Dispute

Forty-five years of Security Council involvement in the Arab-Israeli conflict attest to the continuing importance of dispute settlement efforts in the Middle East and to the problems these efforts may encounter. Throughout the Cold War, a pattern was established whereby the permanent members (in various combinations) worked directly with Israel and the Arabs after each cease-fire to set the ground rules for postwar negotiations; the Security Council then blessed the result, most importantly in Resolution 242 after the June 1967 war.

It has been more than three decades since Resolution 242 was adopted, and it has yet to be fully implemented. Yet it was negotiated with the principal states concerned and later accepted by all the parties to the dispute. The reasons for noncompliance are as complex as the dispute itself. But high on the list has been the backsliding of both sides on key provisions of Resolution 242—and later of Resolution 338—and the unwillingness of the permanent members to insist on compliance.

The problem of giving weight to Security Council recommendations for the resolution of dangerous disputes may be the most difficult aspect of peaceful settlement activity. It is a problem that vexed the founders of the United Nations and one that is inherent in all mediation and conciliation efforts. For if it is neither feasible nor morally defensible to impose settlement terms in the absence of aggression, it is also important that the Security Council be able to see through to agreement guidelines that it negotiates with the parties. In the case of Resolutions 242 and 338, the problem of implementation was intensified by Cold War rivalries. The superpowers rarely joined forces, as they did in Namibia, to urge a common position with both sides. The end of the Cold War does not dispose of the problem, but it opens the door at least to the kind of concerted use of influence that the UN Charter assumes.

The Arab-Israeli dispute is the prototype of the regional conflict that threatens great-power interests and, at one stage or another, engages the Security Council. Because of the lopsided support for the Arab position at the United Nations, the Middle East conflict would seem to be the least likely of all candidates for collective security. In fact, because of the changed dynamics in the Security Council, collective security could play a significant role in its earliest sense of international "guarantees of political independence and territorial integrity to great and small powers alike" (Wilson's Fourteenth Point).

One can see advantages to a permanent-member guarantee of the borders of Israel and the Arab states in conjunction with an overall peace treaty that the parties negotiate. The offer of such a guarantee could serve as an incentive to the parties to take the risks inherent in any final settlement. Once an agreement had been concluded, but before it had been carried out in all its stages, a five-power guarantee could help to promote stability by discouraging rejectionists from disruptive activity aimed at undermining the process.

Territorial guarantees have been applied to the region before. The Tripartite Declaration by Great Britain, France, and the United States of May 25, 1950, helped to maintain peace between Israel and the Arab states for several years. In that declaration, the three governments declared that "should they find that any of these States [the Arab states and Israel] was preparing to violate frontiers or armistice lines," they would "immediately take action, both within and outside the United Nations, to prevent any such violation." The pledge to take action both "outside the United Nations" as well as within it should appeal to both sides. It would meet Israel's need for a U.S. guarantee of immediate action in the event of threatened aggression and that of the Arab states for permanent-member assurances under the rubric of the United Nations.

Would Russia and China be willing to join such a guarantee and, if borders were violated, participate in collective enforcement action? One cannot be sure. But the interests of both in a strong Security Council at the center of world politics calls for a responsible leadership role in this and other issues outside their immediate concern.

8

The Gulf War and Its Implications for an International Deterrent Force

The ten-month crisis in the Persian Gulf (the war, its prelude, and its aftermath) was a defining period for the United Nations. As a form of collective security—minus the UN flag, the implementing mechanisms of the UN Charter, and the obligation of all members to participate in the action if called upon—the Persian Gulf operation helps to clarify the issues by its contrasts as well as its similarities to the UN Charter system. This chapter accordingly looks at some of the main collective-security issues against the backdrop of that crisis. These include the problem of maintaining permanent-member agreement throughout a crisis; the Security Council's authority over the use of force in the absence of standby forces under Article 43; the place of economic sanctions; questions concerning the command and direction of UN forces; and the ways in which a collective-security deterrent force might have been used in the early stages of the crisis.

Post–Cold War Dynamics in the Security Council

The essential procedural requirement for collective security, whether UN Charter–based or of the ad hoc, legitimizing variety, is that the five permanent members agree on fundamental goals and the means to attain them, and that at least four other members of the council are persuaded to vote with them. In the Gulf operation, the new decisionmaking processes that the council developed shortly after the end of the Cold War helped to bring this condition about.

A central feature of the new procedures was a modus operandi that the permanent members began to use toward the end of the Iran-Iraq war: an informal institution known as the Permanent Five.[1] Within this framework, U.S. priorities were first discussed intensively with Great Britain and France, with whom there was generally broad agreement, and then with China and the USSR. Although China frequently waited for a non-aligned position to develop, it tried to avoid acting apart from the other four—a posture plainly influenced by Beijing's isolation after the 1989 events at Tiananmen Square. The Soviet position thus became critical, and considerable time was spent negotiating texts with the USSR and accommodating its views where possible.

Once the Permanent Five had reached agreement, or at least thoroughly discussed a resolution, the text of the resolution would be presented to the other ten members of the Security Council. The three who were not part of the nonaligned bloc generally agreed to the draft. Holding the key then were the seven nonaligned states on the council, who used their swing-vote position to make their views felt. In the end, often after lengthy discussion, most of the nonaligned countries except Cuba and Yemen supported the resolutions, at which point China felt comfortable in giving its final support. The result of this multilevel consultative process was that most resolutions passed by at least three or four votes more than the minimum nine. In this new dynamic, permanent-member cooperation provided the impetus while broad consensus supplied the staying power.

When it became clear that armed force might be needed to bring about Iraq's withdrawal from Kuwait, the question was how—and on what authority—to take military action in the absence of the armed forces contemplated in the UN Charter. Since Article 43 agreements had not been negotiated, UN members were under no obligation to participate in the enforcement action against Iraq. In the Korea crisis of 1950, as we have seen, the Security Council handled the problem by recommending that military contingents be contributed to a unified command under the United States almost immediately after the North Korean invasion occurred. Also, because of Soviet nonparticipation, the council was able to extend the UN mantle over the operation in a way that it was not prepared to repeat in the Gulf.

Legal Authority for the Use of Force Against Iraq

The question of legal authority for the use of force arose early in the Gulf crisis and for several weeks deeply divided the council. At first the issue concerned the right of individual states to use maritime power to enforce the trade sanctions of Resolution 661 without explicit Security Council authorization. The United States maintained that once Kuwait had requested its assistance, it possessed the authority to institute a naval blockade under the right of collective self-defense in Article 51. The other council members, to the contrary, insisted that since Article 51 limits the right of collective self-defense to the period "until the Security Council has taken measures to maintain international peace," the right to act independently of the council ended with the imposition of sanctions.[2]

At this early stage most members also argued that the UN Charter's clear intent is to give nonmilitary sanctions sufficient time to take effect before enforcement action is taken. It is for this reason, they maintained, that Article 42 makes the imposition of military measures contingent upon the council's judgment that nonmilitary measures "would be inadequate or have proved to be inadequate."[3] As it turned out, the council never did formally decide that its economic sanctions would be inadequate; however, it laid the foundation for enforcement action by establishing a pattern of Iraqi disregard for international law in the eleven resolutions it adopted before authorizing the use of offensive force.

Underlying the legal arguments was the basic political issue of the Security Council's control over the progression from economic sanctions to military enforcement. Most council members viewed the language of Article 42 as the key to preserving their influence over events. The United States, on the other hand, was concerned that Security Council authority would not only be hard to obtain but, if granted, might entail unwelcome conditions on the timing and nature of military operations. Yet it soon became clear that the council's authorization of the use of armed force was the key to allied unity and, more broadly, the price of international legitimacy.

It is worth pausing over one of the more conspicuous lessons of the crisis: the difficulty of determining whether economic sanctions would work and of deciding how much time they should be given before moving to enforcement action. In Iraq's case it was clear that the country's ability to withstand outside pressure depended as much on the psychology of the ruler and the interests of the military as it did on the economic consequences of the embargo. Because the effect of the sanctions hinged on these human and group reactions, they were extremely difficult to predict.

Yet economic and political sanctions are an integral part of the UN security system and a useful tool for preventing and defeating aggression. Whether they accomplish the council's objectives depends to a large extent on how closely they can be tailored to the aggressor's vulnerabilities. Generally the tailoring process involves a conspicuous role for countries that are politically and culturally close to the aggressor nation—not only in the application of sanctions and in preventive diplomacy, but in enforcement action if that becomes necessary. Thus the need to engage neighboring powers and political allies of the aggressor becomes paramount. And that is most feasible if regional rapid-deployment forces, formed as part of an international deterrent system, are available to the Security Council on its call in accordance with the provisions of Article 43.

The standoff in the Security Council over the use of force came to an end on August 25, 1990, when the council adopted Resolution 665 authorizing the use of naval power to halt inward and outward shipping in the Gulf. This action not only settled the immediate issue but marked a turning point in U.S. policy: Henceforth the United States would seek UN authority for the use of force and for decisions concerning the nature of the peace. Three months later, in Resolution 678, the council authorized a military offensive if Iraq did not withdraw from Kuwait by January 15, 1991. Together, Resolutions 665 and 678 established a new basis for the use of collective force, combining the overall authority of Chapter VII with specific Security Council authorization for the measures required by the situation. This process departed from the UN Charter because of the absence of the implementing machinery of Chapter VII; nonetheless it provided legitimacy and, in the end, achieved the Security Council's goal of getting Iraq out of Kuwait.

If the ad hoc collective-security operation in the Persian Gulf achieved its objective, should it not provide the model for future enforcement actions? This depends on whether ad hoc alliances are likely to be more or less effective in preventing regional aggression than task forces made up of the rapid-deployment units of an international deterrent force. The Security Council's approach to problems along the way to Iraq's expulsion from Kuwait sheds light on this question.

Issues of Strategic Direction, Command, and Consultations

Article 47 of the UN Charter gives responsibility "for the strategic direction of any armed forces placed at the disposal of the Security Council" to a Military Staff Committee consisting of the permanent members' chiefs of staff or their representatives. During the Gulf crisis, a slightly changed version of the MSC met to organize enforcement of the maritime sanctions under Resolution 665. It played a serviceable, if minor, role in coordinating the flow of military information.

By "strategic direction," the framers of the charter meant to encompass the military planning and direction of large-scale operations. The phrase is used to distinguish between tactical field command on the one hand and overall political control on the other. The concept of a military staff organization flowed directly from the Combined Chiefs of Staff of World War II, whose planning of the allied campaigns was an important factor in the successful conduct of the war. At Dumbarton Oaks the only question about the MSC was whether its membership should be restricted to the permanent members or broadened to include the entire Security Council. Limited membership was agreed upon as most consistent with the committee's functions. Nevertheless, Article 47 leaves open the door to wider participation by providing that any UN member whose participation is required for "the efficient discharge of the Committee's responsibilities" shall be invited to take part in its work.

The MSC, then, was designed to be a military-planning body, subject to the Security Council's mandate and control, without policy responsibilities of its own. The committee does have a significant role to play in the consultation process before the authorization of an enforcement action. By inviting nonpermanent members of the Security Council and military and financial contributors to participate in its deliberations, it can respond to their interest in keeping abreast of the UN operations they support.

It is important to distinguish between institutionalized consultations (through an enlarged MSC or, under Article 44, through participation in the Security Council itself) and informal consultations outside the institutions of the charter. Until the council's permanent membership is enlarged to reflect contemporary power realities, the demands for increased representation are likely to be met mainly through informal consultations among governments. As the Gulf crisis showed, this is the way coalitions are held together in the real world, and there is no reason to suppose that the process would be different in UN Charter–based actions.

The key to the success of a UN military operation is sustained legitimacy. This is as true of ad hoc actions like Desert Storm as it would be for collective-security operations managed through the institutions of Chapter VII. The main constraint on one-nation dictation is the compelling need of the dominant state to maintain consensus, not the consultative mechanisms of collective security. (Had Egypt, Saudi Arabia, Syria, Turkey, and France opposed a drive on Baghdad, would the United States have moved without their support—supposing it had wished to do so?) To those who worry about the constraints that a working MSC or an enlarged Security Council would put on effective military action, the answer is that the constraints are already there, a necessary part of joint operations that depend for their viability on the preservation of consensus.

In addition to its "strategic direction" responsibility, the Military Staff Committee could be given a number of useful tasks in peacetime. It could be used to provide the secretary general and the Security Council with coordinated permanent-member estimates on actual or potential conflicts. The secretary general's military adviser might be invited to participate regularly in these meetings to improve communication between the permanent members and the secretariat on military issues. If an international deterrent force were formed under Article 43, the committee would have a central role to play in coordinating the training and joint maneuvers of the rapid-deployment units. Finally, the MSC might serve as a forum for consideration of the security aspects of regional arms control arrangements, both with the parties to regional disputes and, where appropriate, with regional organizations.

The UN Charter leaves open the question of command responsibility for enforcement actions. The issue has never been seriously addressed, much less resolved, because the Cold War relieved UN members of the need to do so. The United States did study the issue internally in 1944 and concluded that one approach would be to decide on command arrangements for each enforcement operation at the time of need.[4] Today this still seems the simplest and most practicable course. The result would be that the principal military contributor in each operation would assume the responsibility for its command.

That the command of multinational operations is more complicated than unilateral command is clear; that it is possible is also apparent from the military alliances of two world wars and other coalitions throughout history. The contributors to a UN operation are more politically heterogeneous than most coalition partners and, in some cases, less directly threatened by the aggression. This makes it doubly important that the states participating in a UN action agree from the outset on the objectives of the operation, the military means to carry them out, and the conditions of termination. In ad hoc as in charter-based collective-security actions, the selection of coalition members is a process left primarily to the state in command of the force.

Ad Hoc Coalitions Versus Charter-Based
UN Deterrent Forces

Any discussion of the formation of an international deterrent force under the provisions of Chapter VII must compare that system to its main alternative: the ad hoc, UN-authorized alliance, as employed in Korea and the Gulf. Arguments can be made for both positions.

The case for the ad hoc approach rests partly on a natural inclination to avoid fixing something that does not seem broken. The U.S.-led coalition worked in the Gulf crisis, it is argued, and different coalitions can be formed to meet different circumstances in the future. Why buy trouble? Article 43 agreements would be hard to negotiate. Some states might insist on escape clauses that permitted them to opt out of operations they opposed, vitiating the purpose of the exercise. The obligation to use UN standby forces could inhibit unilateral action when it was needed. Despite the U.S. veto, an Article 43 agreement between the United States and the Security Council could raise the specter of supranationalism when submitted to the Senate for ratification. Finally, if states are willing to participate in a UN operation, they do not need a special agreement to do so. They will take part because their interests are at stake, not because of legal commitments.

This case rests on the sometimes unrecognized assumption that the United States will provide the leadership for future UN enforcement actions, as it did in Korea and the Gulf. It is an assumption that is doubtless correct for serious threats to U.S. vital interests. Only the United States has the military power to deal with major aggression, and no one else at century's end is capable of assuming the leadership of global coalitions. But what of the majority of the world's conflicts that have relatively little bearing on U.S. interests? Few Americans are prepared to see their country take on a disproportionate share of the burden in these conflicts. In part, this is a recognition that the United States no longer has the resources to play such a role in light of pressing domestic needs. More fundamentally, it is a sense that the costs in human lives and finances should be paid primarily by the states that benefit from the actions.

What then is to be done about the conflicts between small, strategically unimportant countries that few people care about except those involved? If these quarrels are left to be settled by improvised UN coalitions, most of them will not be settled at all. Indeed, most cases of regional aggression will be over before the UN can respond. That may not adversely affect the short-term interests of the major powers, but it cannot be mistaken for a stable world order.

But is it realistic in a world of competing national interests to expect UN members to carry out the commitments of Article 43 today, even if those obligations are less onerous than those they accepted when joining the United Nations? There is no way to know for certain until the members are asked and the positions of respected and powerful nations become clear. Nevertheless, there are several ways in which UN members might be persuaded to accept the core obligations of collective security.

At the top of the list is a declaration by the permanent members that no state would be required to contribute to enforcement actions outside its region and without effect on its interests. In addition, the permanent members could encourage the participation of others in a collective-security system by pledging to make their own forces available when they vote to establish an enforcement action. This commitment would not apply to an abstention and it would not stand in the way of the veto. In the Gulf crisis abstention made sense for China: Beijing did not wish to take part in the operation but neither did it have any reason to veto its establishment.

Whatever the declarations of the permanent members, the problem remains of persuading sovereign states to commit themselves to military action at the direction of others. Are there incentives that could be offered to encourage the negotiation of Article 43 agreements for a collective-security deterrent force? Three possibilities come to mind:

1. Financial assistance to poorer states to help them develop the forces designated in their Article 43 agreements.
2. Rapid-deployment training with air transport and special-forces units of the permanent members.
3. Provision of modern arms and equipment for the rapid-deployment units of those UN members that need such assistance in order to carry out their functions in an international deterrent force.

States unable to provide combat forces could be offered the option of furnishing communications, logistics, or field hospital units. Once momentum developed, international respectability would almost certainly come into play. To make sure it did, rotating membership in the Security Council could be tied to a member's willingness to negotiate Article 43 agreements and to provide the designated units when its interests were engaged. (It is so tied now, in theory, under Article 23, which provides that in the election of nonpermanent members "due regard [shall be] specially paid . . . to the contribution of Members . . . to the maintenance of international peace and security.")

Smaller powers could be encouraged to contribute to a global security system through the development of more effective regional security bodies. The UN Charter strikes a balance between the need to involve the concerned states of a region in enforcement actions and the need for the Security Council to maintain control of the actions. Article 53 directs the council to utilize, where appropriate, "regional arrangements or agencies for enforcement action under its authority"; however, it adds that "no enforcement action shall be taken . . . by regional agencies without the authorization of the Security Council."

Active regional participation is essential to a collective-security deterrent system. The credibility of the system depends on the military contributions of small and middle powers, but equally important is the Security Council's ability to respond to threats of aggression without lengthy deliberations with the regional bodies. One way of handling the problem would be to create small security committees within the regional organizations, authorized to consult with the Security Council on possible enforcement actions if time permitted. Such consultations would not preclude direct communication between the Security Council and the individual states of the region, and the positions of the regional security committees would not affect the right of individual states to participate in the IDF actions they supported.

As a practical matter, the present state of regional organization some-times makes it difficult or impossible to rely on regional groups for secu-rity purposes. In some cases the potential aggressor may be the dominant power in the region; in others the victim may be an outcast, requiring the Security Council to act without the support of regional states. The re-gional bodies also vary greatly in effectiveness from one area to another. In some areas, notably in Latin America and occasionally in Africa, they have at times worked fairly well, sometimes in tandem with the United Nations. In the North Atlantic community, NATO's ACE Mobile Force has the capacity to act with great speed and power. Elsewhere, regional security bodies are moribund or ineffective, and in South and East Asia they do not exist. It is possible that the process of creating an interna-tional deterrent system would increase the involvement of smaller pow-ers in their own security as they train the contingents they agree to make available to the Security Council.

The Uses of an International Deterrent System in the Gulf Crisis

The Persian Gulf crisis is a classic case of rising tensions coupled with un-certainty about a potential aggressor's intentions. It is a situation in which individual states are reluctant to intervene by themselves, espe-cially when the threatened state is unwilling to ask for military help, as Kuwait was at first. After Iraq invaded, the U.S.-led coalition responded in good time, considering the preparations needed to drive Iraq out of territory it had had six months to fortify. Had the United States acted uni-laterally before the attack, however, it would have been widely con-demned for overreacting to what was generally viewed as Iraqi bluster in an oil-pricing dispute.

In contrast, if an international deterrent system had been in place, the Security Council would have had several options immediately available. At the first indication of Iraqi maneuvers along the Kuwait border, the council could have placed on alert a task force of Arab and Islamic pow-ers and the concerned permanent members. The Military Staff Commit-tee, as disseminator of the alert, would have made certain Iraq was aware of the planned composition of the task force that would oppose it. Simul-taneously, air transport units that had trained with the regional IDF con-tingents would have been sent to the area. If Iraq had threatened to attack despite these actions, the council could have then deployed advance ele-ments of the task force along Kuwait's northern frontier. Meanwhile, permanent-member air and naval units would have deployed in and around the Gulf as an "over-the-horizon" deterrent. As these military placements went ahead, the Security Council could have dispatched a mediation team to Baghdad consisting of representatives of the IDF task-force states and possibly the secretary general's office. There would have been no mistake in Saddam Hussein's mind about the nature of the opposition he would face in invading Kuwait.

In the early stages of a crisis like that in the Gulf, one of the strongest weapons of preventive diplomacy is the no-fault determination that blames no one for the crisis and avoids the political thicket of taking sides. Under Article 40, the council is authorized to take "such provisional measures as it deems necessary . . . without prejudice to the rights . . . of the parties concerned." This path may be disingenuous at times, but it opens doors to mediation and leaves the potential aggressor an exit that is not humiliating. It is also the answer to difficult cases like the Vietnamese invasion of Cambodia and the Iraqi invasion of Iran, in which complicating events before the invasion make it difficult to form a strong UN coalition.

The IDF system allows for a graduated system of deterrents, which, from the Security Council's first move, signals the composition of the UN force and the council's determination to defeat the threatened aggression.[5] It puts maximum pressure on the potential aggressor to negotiate and gives him the least amount of time to reinforce his position on the ground. The deployment of advance units in this sequence can be extremely fast. In peacekeeping operations that have been pressed by the permanent members, UN troops have been on the ground in the Middle East within twelve hours of Security Council authorization—even without the existence of rapid-deployment units.[6]

In the Gulf crisis, other advantages would have flowed from the existence of an international deterrent force. The participating contingents would have trained together and worked out the command-and-control problems inherent in multinational operations. The Security Council would have had available to it bases, supply depots, and rights of passage negotiated under Article 43. The costs of the operation would have been borne collectively by UN members, a matter of some importance if the victim does not happen to be an oil-producing kingdom. In short, there would have been a credible military deterrent to back up the diplomatic efforts to settle the dispute peacefully.

A deterrent task force like the one hypothesized for the Gulf crisis has three characteristics central to effective collective security. The military burden is shared by countries with the greatest interest in the settlement; the initial tripwire operation is defensive unless challenged; and the regional and permanent-member forces together represent such an overwhelming deterrent that the likelihood of combat is extremely low.

9

Somalia and the Ambiguities of Peace Enforcement

In the gray area between collective security and traditional peacekeeping that has characterized the most sensitive UN missions since the Gulf war, the Somalia crisis was the first to test the limits of armed humanitarian action in internal conflicts. The starvation, disease, and civil war that wracked Somalia in the early 1990s were, above all, an agonizing human tragedy. But they also provided a testing ground for the view that the United Nations could, and should, intervene with armed force in internal humanitarian disasters—even if the domestic turmoil posed no serious threat to the security of other states. This view assumes a broader right of intervention in "matters which are essentially within the domestic jurisdiction of [states]" than that envisaged in Article 2, paragraph 7 of the charter.

After the UN's difficulties in Somalia the mood shifted again, from the buoyant internationalism of the early post–Cold War years to a narrower construction of the right of intervention. Yet the debate is far from over. In fact, it seems likely to intensify so long as the greater part of the world's violence stems from civil war rather than international conflict. Of the ninety-odd cases of armed struggle that have erupted around the world since 1989, more than eighty have been domestic conflicts, and of these the UN has been directly or indirectly involved in over half.[1] These civil wars have involved more than 175 national groups and organizations, reflecting a world in which less than 10 percent of the states are ethnically homogeneous.[2]

Somalia is one of the 10 percent. The warfare that devastated the country in the early 1990s stemmed not from ethnic or religious antagonism but from a struggle for power among the clan-based factions of a failed state—factions that shared a common racial and linguistic heritage and a history of relative peace with each other. The power-and-interest factors that have driven the fighting in Somalia stand in contrast to the ethnic animosity that has fueled the intercommunal conflicts in countries like Burundi, Rwanda, and Cyprus. One would expect that a power-based conflict would be more likely to end in a settlement than a war fueled by racism and religious bigotry. In Somalia that has not happened. Three years after the last UN troops pulled out in 1995, there is still no central government, the ports of the capital remain closed, the fighting continues, and twenty-six different factions control various pieces of the country.

The UN peacekeeping mission in Somalia occurred in three phases. Each involved a different level of authorized force, a different command structure, and a different approach to the principles of impartiality and consent. The first phase, a traditional UN-directed peacekeeping action in which the use of force was limited to self-defense, had little success against the opposition of heavily armed Somali warlords. That operation, the UN Operation in Somalia (UNOSOM I) is of interest mainly in reinforcing the obvious: that the Cold War guidelines for consensual peacekeeping do not apply to conflicts in which the belligerents, or some of them at least, are opposed to UN involvement. In contrast, phases two and three of the intervention (the United Task Force [UNITAF] and UNOSOM II) were launched and carried out under Chapter VII of the UN Charter. The chief difference between UNITAF and UNOSOM II concerned their direction and command responsibilities. UNITAF, like the UN operations in Korea and the Gulf, was authorized by the Security Council but directed and commanded by the United States. UNOSOM II, on the other hand, was the first use of force under Chapter VII to fall unequivocally under the direction of the secretary general.

The Impact of the Cold War

The historical context for the UN intervention in Somalia can be briefly reviewed. The magnitude of the civil violence that began to spread through the country in 1988 stemmed partly from the abrupt change in Somalia's position from Cold War pawn to strategic backwater. Historically, Somalia has been the consolation prize in the Horn of Africa, overshadowed by Ethiopia during the colonial era as well as the Cold War. After taking power in 1969, Mohamed Siad Barre strengthened an already close military relationship with the Soviet Union, his first goal being the reintegration of land that had once been part of "Greater Somalia." This included Djibouti and northern Kenya, where ethnic Somalis still formed the majority, but the main objective of Somali nationalists was the large area in eastern Ethiopia known as the Ogaden. In 1977 Siad Barre invaded the Ogaden and was roundly defeated. To add to Siad Barre's problems, King Haile Selassie of Ethiopia was overthrown at about the same time by a Marxist military junta led by Mengistu Haile Mariam, whereupon the Soviets reversed alliances and installed themselves in Addis Ababa. The circle closed two years later, as the fall of the shah of Iran and the Soviet invasion of Afghanistan led Washington to take a new look at the narrow band of arid land across from the oil fields of the Arabian peninsula.

Somalia's strategic importance to the United States in the 1980s lay primarily in its suitability as a staging area for the defense of the Persian Gulf. Commanding access to the Bab el-Mandeb Strait and the Red Sea, the U.S. air and naval facilities at Berbera were part of a network of bases that gave substance to the "Carter doctrine" that the security of the area was vital to the United States and that U.S. allies in the region would be protected from aggression. In return for the base rights, Washington launched a sizable economic development program in Somalia (by 1985 the second largest in sub-Saharan Africa) and a more limited array of military assistance projects.

The courtship of Somalia by the superpowers affected the crisis of the early 1990s in two ways. The most significant was that the country was awash in arms. Although the weapons may have been too old to win a foreign war, they were well suited to terrorizing the populace and prolonging the fighting among the clans. Missiles, rockets, and machine guns became the currency of power. Their importance to the warlords' position in the struggle for power made disarmament more difficult, and their quantity and wide distribution increased the risk of guerrilla attacks against UN troops.

The Security Council tried to get a grip on the arms problem in early 1992 by establishing a "complete embargo on all deliveries of weapons and military equipment to Somalia"—a good example of closing the barn door after the horse has already escaped.[3] The most urgent requirement was not to prevent future arms deliveries but to reduce the number of weapons in circulation. That, however, entailed demilitarization of the clans, an undertaking that the United States was not ready to embark upon. The issue of disarmament divided Washington and UN headquarters in New York throughout the crisis. Secretary General Boutros Boutros-Ghali pressed for demilitarization to ensure a relatively safe environment for the defensively armed UN peacekeeping force that was expected to follow UNITAF and UNOSOM II. The United States refused to endanger the lives of its own troops in a humanitarian mission to protect the delivery of relief supplies. The conflicting interests were institutional and perhaps inevitable. They arose in part from the ambiguities of "peace enforcement," which are explored later in this chapter.

The second effect of the Cold War was Siad Barre's continuation in power, with the support of the United States, well beyond the point when he would normally have been overthrown. "Increasingly authoritarian, reclusive, and senile . . . the dictator found himself mayor only of Mogadishu [when] on January 26, 1991, he was chased from his capital by a people in arms."[4] The pent-up frustrations of the tribal competitors for power contributed to the intensity of the violence and the utter collapse of the state after Siad Barre's fall. In Somalia, as in other Cold War satellites, superpower support against external threats came with an internal security relationship that tended to freeze political change and maintain incumbents in power. By the late 1980s, the special U.S. relationship with the Siad Barre regime had all but ended, a victim of the post-Soviet power configuration and U.S. human rights concerns. When agreements for use of the Berbera facilities came up for extension in 1988, Washington declined to renew them, "Siad Barre's genocidal depredations in the northwest [having] made continuation of the agreements out of the question."[5]

Like the Persian Gulf war, which erupted at about the same time, the conflict in Somalia was shaped by its peculiar time and circumstances. In important respects it was just as unique as the Persian Gulf crisis. A perceptive Somali observer remarked at the time that the complete collapse of the state in 1992 was unprecedented in scope, at least since World War II. He concluded that only "Liberia provides a somewhat similar example; however, the capital city, Monrovia, never fell into rebel hands."[6] It seems likely that most future humanitarian crises—even those that are militarily induced—will not be fueled by as many weapons, fought by as many factions, or played out in quite so anarchic a situation as Somalia.

To say that the Cold War had a destabilizing effect on Somalia is not to suggest that the country was otherwise free of the self-destructive patterns then evident in other sub-Saharan nations. By the early 1990s, the problems characteristic of failed or failing states could be found in most of Somalia's communal activities. In domestic politics, the democratic experiment that had marked the first nine years of independence had totally failed. Outside Siad Barre's Marehan clan, which was the government's principal base of power, an alienated society expected nothing but trouble from the government, and got it. In the economy, a barely subsistent combination of nomadism and small-scale entrepreneurship collapsed under the warlords' depredations in the countryside and the massive destruction of the capital. Economic stagnation led in turn to high unemployment among young males and their easy recruitment by the belligerents.

Meanwhile, the Somali clan system had become dysfunctional. As a Somali observer noted at the time, the communal violence that in other parts of the post–Cold War world followed "ethnic, racial, linguistic or religious cleavages" was "in Somalia . . . channeled along clan lines."[7]

The fighting among the clans involved sustained, systematic assaults by the militias of one clan against the unarmed civilians of another. What is most striking is that nothing in the country's history foreshadowed such uncontrolled violence. Somalia had been a "singularly homogeneous culture" without significant ethnic or religious minorities, whose five main clan families had coexisted for centuries without unusual discord.[8]

The descent into savage war when the constraints of government are removed and the products of labor denied is not a new, or uniquely African, phenomenon. It was described by a British philosopher some 350 years ago: "During the time men live without a common Power to keep them all in awe, they are in that condition which is called War; and such a war is of every man, against every man. . . . In such condition there is no place for Industry, because the fruit thereof is uncertain: and consequently . . . no Arts; no Letters; no Society; and, which is worst of all, continual fear and danger of violent death."[9]

Distributing Humanitarian Relief Against Armed Opposition

The Scope of the Disaster and the Early UN Response

The three UN peacekeeping actions in Somalia, with their varying force levels and distinct command structures, were all attempts to respond to the same problem: how to get food and medicine to starving people against the armed obstruction of warring gangs in a nonfunctioning state. These operations were the first to use collective force for strictly humanitarian purposes. In doing so they broke new ground, raising issues on the uses of UN force that differ from those involved in defeating aggression or monitoring cease-fire lines. To understand the ways in which force was applied in Somalia—and to be able to judge whether alternative paths exist that could have accomplished the relief job with fewer foreign-policy risks—the first step is to look at the relief situation in early 1992 when the UN secretariat became actively involved in the crisis.

The initial UN involvement combined efforts to facilitate the delivery of relief supplies with negotiations aimed at ending the war. In March 1992, through the efforts of UN Under Secretary General James Jonah, a cease-fire was accepted by the main factions in Mogadishu, leaving General Mohamed Farah Aideed in control of the south of the city and his chief rival, Ali Mahdi, in control of the north. This agreement was honored, albeit intermittently and without the association of the freelance gangs, until the arrival of UNITAF in late 1992.[10] Also active during the spring of 1992 was the secretary general's special representative, Mohamed Sahnoun, who consulted with faction leaders and community elders to lay the groundwork for a political settlement. Sahnoun's approach, like that of U.S. Special Envoy Robert Oakley after him, was to seek the warlords' consent to the deployment of UN forces and the distribution of relief.[11] Consent, however, proved a slippery commodity. Although often granted, it was just as often withdrawn when a new military balance changed the interests of the factions or the UN secretariat was perceived as acting from partisan motives.

The diplomatic initiatives of the UN were buttressed throughout the conflict by the efforts of various Western, Islamic, and African powers, working independently and together. For example, President Meles Zinawi of Ethiopia, representing the Horn of Africa Committee of the Organization of African Unity (OAU), played an important part in organizing the national reconciliation conference that was held in Addis Ababa in January 1993.[12] Some of the regional and great-power initiatives made progress on limited measures like temporary cease-fires, heavy-weapons containment, and steps toward power sharing in a reconstructed state. The diplomatic side of the Somalia crisis is outside the scope of this chapter, yet it should be kept in mind that for three years peaceful-settlement activities were concurrent with UN military efforts to facilitate the delivery of relief supplies.

In the Somalia crisis, as in many deteriorating situations, opportunities for mediation existed in the early stages of the conflict that were no longer available after the violence spread. To many of those involved, it seemed self-evident that the time for effective diplomacy was before the hostilities turned into full-scale civil war.[13] Sahnoun describes three occasions—in 1988, 1989, and 1991—when the UN failed to respond to calls from within the country and the region for help in national reconciliation. At these points, he argues, a UN mediation effort might have been successful if supported by the deployment of a small, well-trained security force that could protect the relief efforts. But no such force was available. There is no way of knowing whether a combination of vigorous early diplomacy and enhanced internal security could have prevented the descent into total war. The most that can be said is that well-trained African rapid-deployment units, backed by permanent-member forces and conveyed by transport units of a deterrent task force they had trained with, would have provided a preventive option that did not exist.

In January 1992, when the Security Council first took action to help deliver humanitarian aid to Somalis in need of it, the famine had already reached biblical dimensions. When Sahnoun arrived in March on a fact-finding mission for the secretary general, he found that "at least 300,000 people had died of hunger and hunger-related disease, and thousands more were casualties of the repression and the civil war."[14] In the south-central region, which had suffered most from the scorched-earth practices of Siad Barre and Aideed, more than half the population had perished. Marauding armed bands destroyed much of the livestock and cultivation, and in the interior medical care had virtually ceased to exist. Meanwhile, as agricultural production fell to about half the normal yield, more than 400,000 Somalis fled to refugee camps in Ethiopia, Kenya, and Djibouti.

The magnitude of the disaster in early 1992 is central to any discussion of the progression from peacekeeping, through emergency airlifts, to enforcement action. In April the hard policy choices that lay ahead began with an uncontroversial Security Council decision to establish a UN peacekeeping force and observer group for Somalia (UNOSOM I).[15] This operation had a brief and checkered career. Launched with the consent of the concerned parties, denied permission to enter Somalia in June because of Aideed's animosity toward the UN, and finally dispatched when Aideed withdrew his objections, the five-hundred-man Pakistani unit arrived in September only to remain secluded for months in barracks near the Mogadishu airport. The force commander had simply concluded that his contingent lacked the means to carry out its mandate against the thousand or so young gunmen who opposed it.

The mandate of this small peacekeeping force was indeed formidable. Governed by rules of engagement that permitted the use of force only in self-defense, UNOSOM I was meant to secure the port, ensure the safe passage of food shipments from the airport, and escort convoys from the harbor to distribution points in Mogadishu. All this was to be done in a power context in which the interests of some of the most powerful elements lay in preventing the UN from carrying out these tasks. Indeed, the armed groups that blocked the deployment of the force—not all of them answerable to Aideed and the other warlords—were the same people who distributed the food at extortionate rates when they did not actually steal it.

The Role of Nongovernmental Organizations in Insurgency-Based Disasters

Recognizing the need for additional contingents, the Security Council approved the enlargement of UNOSOM I by 3,500 troops in late August 1992, although it did not change the rules of engagement.[16] As it turned out, the new units were never dispatched. In part, this was because the emergency airlift that had been recommended by the secretary general and endorsed by the Security Council[17] was already delivering food to areas in the "triangle of death" west of Mogadishu. The U.S. airlift, known as Operation Provide Relief, worked in tandem with humanitarian relief personnel on the ground, many of them provided by nongovernmental organizations (NGOs), which tended to be better represented in the interior than the UN agencies.[18] Among the NGOs working in Somalia when the airlift began to fly out of Kenya were CARE, SOS International, Irish Concern, Médecins sans Frontières, Save the Children UK, the International Medical Corps, and the International Committee of the Red Cross (ICRC), the latter four having remained in the country throughout the crisis.[19] These organizations identified the areas in greatest need of food and medicine, furnished information on security conditions at the airstrips and airdrop locations, and picked up and delivered the supplies to distribution points in the interior.

The NGOs were on the scene before, during, and after the crisis became the focus of international attention and high policy. For Operation Provide Relief they represented a mine of experience and established relationships in the countryside. Indeed, one of the lessons of Somalia is the centrality of these groups to the conduct of effective relief operations in insurgency-based disasters. They are willing, first of all, to operate under dangerous conditions in which the UN itself feels compelled to transfer the offices of its own humanitarian agencies for reasons of safety.[20] They are often more cost-effective than the UN specialized agencies with their large headquarters staffs (UNICEF being a notable exception). They have internal lines of authority that are more direct and more functional than the links that loosely tie the specialized agencies with the central UN organs. When disaster strikes, it is to the NGOs that most concerned people contribute, giving their work a direct human connection and singleness of purpose that the publicly financed agencies are hard put to match. And, finally, their operation in war-torn countries is less dependent on the vagaries of foreign policy, media attention, and differing member-state interests than the relief agencies of the major powers and the UN.

An example of the problems faced by UN relief agencies is the difficult adjustment that the UN World Food Program (WFP) had to make in August 1992 when the United States decided to give top priority to famine relief in Somalia. The new U.S. policy led to the release of 145,000 metric tons of food for Somalia, about eight times the total amount distributed by the WFP during the first half of 1992.[21] The logistics of suddenly delivering contributions of this magnitude were difficult for a UN agency with limited resources. Non-UN agencies like CARE, Catholic Relief Services, and the ICRC (which distributed most of the U.S. food) were able to adapt more easily to the new levels because of their greater reliance on a relatively stable flow of private funding.

If policy considerations affect the work of the relief agencies, they pale beside the political and financial pressures that influence a decision to intervene militarily in a humanitarian crisis. In Somalia permanent-member interests and concerns presented the Security Council with a choice between taking short-term military action or none at all. Here, as well as in other sub-Saharan crises, the civil violence that accompanies the collapse of marginal states invites a fast-in, fast-out approach—a search for the quick fix that avoids the financial costs of prolonged peace-keeping and the political costs of entanglement. In Somalia the result was a progression from ineffective UN peacekeeping to a powerful but time-limited military operation more suited to fighting aggression than dealing with a humanitarian disaster.

Logistical Aid as an Alternative to the Use of Force

Before turning to the problems of peace enforcement actions, it is worth looking at the effect on the famine of the emergency airlifts provided by the United States and other states and agencies.[22] How successful was this logistical assistance in getting food through to the interior and in circumventing the looting of relief supplies by the competing factions? Was large-scale military intervention essential to the delivery of vital supplies in December 1992 in light of the previous four months' experience with the distribution of food by air? Our standard of success will not be the high level of physical security that heavily armed escorts can provide to relief convoys for a short time. Success will be measured rather by the extent to which logistical aid in a well-coordinated relief program can turn around a cycle of famine and violence while avoiding the problems of armed involvement in a civil war.

Any attempt to gauge the effectiveness of the logistical aid faces a complicating factor. In the late summer and fall of 1992, at the same time that the airlifts became fully operational, the total amount of food from abroad rose sharply. For the first time since the famine began, the supply of humanitarian relief began to meet the most basic demands of the disaster. The explanation for the new donations is clear. In late July, events conspired to make the suffering of the Somali people prime-time news throughout the world. The most striking and widely reported of these events was Secretary General Boutros-Ghali's angry reproof to the members of the Security Council for "fighting a rich man's war in Yugoslavia while not lifting a finger to save Somalia from disintegration."[23] Congressional pressure on the Bush administration to take action also reached its peak at this time, as Senators Paul Simon and Nancy Kassebaum introduced a resolution urging the dispatch of UN forces—if necessary without the consent of the warring factions.[24] Finally, Sahnoun's public information campaign and the bleak reports from the relief community led to extensive media coverage, most notably by the *New York Times* and Cable News Network (CNN).

Clearly Somalia was on the receiving end of a powerful new dynamic in world politics and disaster relief: the capacity of the media to direct attention to any one of the many disasters that occur every day throughout the world—and not necessarily the most urgent one. The media's power to influence relief priorities may be deplored as an inefficient form of triage or welcomed as a source of needed contributions. What is clear is that in Somalia's case the extensive coverage of the famine ushered in a more activist U.S. policy—a policy in which armed intervention was to play a central part.

The Impact of Private and Government Donations

The international response to Somalia's tragedy was fast and generous. Contributions poured in from concerned governments, from private donations to the NGOs, and from the UN disaster relief agencies. Because the increased donations occurred at the same time that the airlifts were becoming most effective, it is hard to measure the impact of the logistical aid alone. The pertinent question is whether *together* the airlifts and the increased food donations had ended the downward cycle of starvation and disease before the forces of UNITAF arrived in December 1992.

To determine the extent of the changes brought about by the airlift, we must look first at the relief situation in Somalia before Operation Provide Relief began to operate out of Mombasa in August 1992. The famine was then at its worst. Sahnoun reported to the secretary general in June 1992 that "less than half of the minimum of 50,000 metric tons [per month] of different food items [that] is needed urgently" had been pledged, much less delivered.[25] Compounding the difficulty of inadequate supplies, he continued, was the lack of progress in creating food distribution networks into the interior. Sahnoun did not dismiss the security problems but considered them closely related to the scarcity of food and the inability to deliver the available supplies to those in need. "An absence of food breeds insecurity," he was to write later, "which, in turn, causes instability leading to starvation, suffering and disease. Breaking this diabolical and vicious cycle may be the key to resolving the intricate social and political problems in Somalia."[26]

At about this time, WFP Director Trevor Page provided an equally stark appraisal of the relief situation. "Because we've let things simmer without paying attention," he said, "[and] because of the disorganization of the United Nations, less than a third of the food that is needed [has] been delivered."[27] Indeed, by mid-July the WFP itself had delivered less than 19,000 of the 68,388 metric tons it had pledged in January.

Some of the food shortfall and distribution problems were plainly due to defects in the UN humanitarian-relief system. The contrasting record of the ICRC in Somalia speaks volumes. According to the Office of U.S. Foreign Disaster Assistance (OFDA) in August 1992, "the ICRC has delivered over 79,000 metric tons of food to Somalia, [although] the effort has been straining ICRC resources."[28] The ICRC brought in its supplies "through twenty different entry points, by sea, by air, and overland across the Kenya-Somalia border. [It] operated 400 kitchens . . . handled the distribution of food to several hospitals in various cities and sustained four daily rotations of airlift delivery from Mombasa, Kenya, to Mogadishu, Belet Uen, and Baidoa."[29] During this massive relief effort, the ICRC suffered one casualty from a ricocheted bullet and encountered no crippling security problems.[30]

In Somalia, the ICRC reportedly bent its long-established rule of rejecting military protection from all sources, whether governments, multinational forces, or rebel groups.[31] To preserve the ICRC's impartiality, the rule extends to vehicles carrying its provisions and bearing its insignia, which are not permitted to be armed. Like the other relief agencies in Mogadishu (but less regularly than most), the ICRC reportedly purchased the services of the so-called "technicals," Somali gunmen who offered the "technical" assistance of their jeep escorts to ensure their clients' safety—presumably from other "technicals." This unsavory protection racket provided the faction leaders and their forces with a steady source of income in exchange for allowing the relief groups to do their jobs.

To Sahnoun it seemed that one way to weaken the power of the gunmen was to foster a more secure climate through the creation of a national police force.[32] The idea had to be abandoned in mid-1992 because of the obvious impracticality of using lightly armed policemen to maintain order while a civil war was in progress. In early 1993, however, following UNITAF's arrival and the temporary unemployment of the armed gangs, the UN did fund and deploy interim Somali police units in Mogadishu and other population centers.[33] Although these units did not play a major role, they eased the day-to-day frictions among people who had just stopped fighting each other—a job clearly more suited to trained policemen than to line troops, no matter how thorough their peacekeeping training.

In some places, such as Cyprus, Namibia, and the Iran-Iraq border, the UN has deployed police officers from outside states to assist the infantry or observer contingents. These civil police units have had success in functions like crowd control, criminal investigation, arrest, and imprisonment. And where war criminals are a part of the scene, as in Bosnia, military police have occasionally (and after intense debate) been used to seize and arrest indicted individuals.[34] Whether national or foreign in composition, police units depend for their effectiveness on the absence of uncontrollable dissident elements. In Somalia, this condition was problematic or nonexistent throughout most of the three UN interventions.

Changes in the Relief Situation Before
UNITAF's Deployment

Returning to the impact of the airlifts and the increased relief supplies on the state of the famine, let us look at the food and security situation two months into Operation Provide Relief. On October 12, 1992, Sahnoun told a donors' conference in Geneva that "only two months ago, we succeeded in penetrating the interior remote areas of Somalia thanks to the airlift operation."[35] "The massive operations that have been launched in the past two months," he continued, ". . . [have] made a tremendous difference in our response to the immediate needs of the starving population. . . . Increased amounts of food and supplementary feeding supplies to the South of Somalia [have reached] an average of 20,000 metric tons a month . . . more than double the quantity supplied before the month of August."[36] A few weeks after this report, the effect of the increased deliveries became apparent in Baidoa as "the number of dead recorded weekly . . . shrank from 1,780 on September 6 to 335 on November 1."[37]

Despite these changes, food distribution remained well below the estimated minimum need of 50,000 metric tons. To close the gap, Sahnoun proposed a "Hundred-Day Plan for Accelerated Assistance." The plan included an ambitious program of increased food aid, expansion of feeding stations in the interior, wider provision of health care, and distribution of seeds, tools, and animal vaccines to revive the agricultural sector. Although Sahnoun did not oppose the insertion of UN peacekeeping troops in principle, the hundred-day plan was designed to end the cycle of famine and violence without resorting to large-scale military involvement.

Looting remained a problem at this time, but there are varying estimates of its extent. NGO estimates of stolen supplies in the fall of 1993 varied "from 30 to 50 percent for most NGOs . . . [to] about 10 percent . . . for the ICRC, the greatest importer of food aid."[38] In October Sahnoun told participants at the donors' conference that "looting is estimated at 15 percent of delivered supplies [for grains], while for high-quality items [such as sugar, rice, and cooking oils], the percentage can be as high as 40 percent."[39] Sahnoun was to write later that "estimates of the amount of food being stolen ranged now from 10 percent to 80 percent," adding that "the U.S. government used the higher figure as part of the justification for Operation Restore Hope."[40]

It is true that some U.S. officials whose firsthand experience and objectivity are equal to Sahnoun's differ with him on the airlift's impact on the famine and the security situation. For example, Robert Oakley writes that the "large-scale airlift of food by the U.S. Air Force . . . had little effect, and death from civil/clan war, famine, and disease continued."[41] And again, "it quickly became apparent that even a sustained airlift would have too low a rate of effectiveness to reverse the situation. The cost quickly became prohibitive . . . and most food never reached the intended NGO or UN beneficiaries."[42]

The sources cited for the latter statements are OFDA situation reports for September 1992 through January 1993. My reading of the OFDA reports is different; in fact I find it hard to discern in them a pattern of any kind. In the May 1992 situation report, before the airlift began, the UN is cited as the source for an "estimate that 4.5 million people in Somalia are facing the threat of starvation."[43] From June 1992 to January 1993, every one of the OFDA reports cites an ICRC estimate that "1.5 million people in Somalia are facing the threat of starvation due to the effects of civil strife."[44] Then, in February and March 1993, after UNITAF's activity had become an important factor, OFDA returns to the UN as its source for an estimate that "2 million people remain at great risk."[45] As for the statement that "the cost [of the airlift] quickly became prohibitive," the cost of the U.S. military operation in Somalia was thirty-four times that of the airlift, or $476 million for the former[46] as against $14 million for the latter.[47]

OFDA officials who handled the U.S. disaster-relief program for Somalia in 1992 offer a more nuanced description of the unfolding relief situation than the situation reports. Their consensus is that by December, when UNITAF deployed, "the situation had stabilized,"[48] and that partly through natural causes "the famine had essentially run its course by the end of the year."[49] They emphasize, however, that this was not entirely clear at the time, and that people in OFDA, Africa Watch, and the NGOs differed among themselves as to the impact of the increased food deliveries.

On balance, it seems fair to conclude that the continuing violence in late 1992 warranted an assessment that armed intervention was still needed for the prompt delivery of vital supplies—albeit intervention on a lesser scale and with different use-of-force arrangements from those of UNITAF and UNOSOM II. But decisions with important political-military implications are not made on the basis of humanitarian considerations alone. A judgment to move into a civil war—no matter how altruistic the motive—must take account of the domestic and international repercussions of the action. In this case, the U.S. decision to intervene with major force, with its inevitable casualties, was to limit later U.S. options in the regional crises that followed the withdrawal from Somalia.

To consider the logistical alternatives to armed intervention is not to minimize the humanitarian achievements of the UN missions in Somalia—achievements that can be measured in lives saved, health restored, and widespread suffering relieved. Instead, its purpose is to show that even the most difficult insurgency-based disasters can be handled with reasonable efficiency through large-scale logistical aid in a well-supplied relief program. It is also a reminder that institutions with long experience in relief work exist in the NGOs and the UN agencies, and that these organizations are able to work effectively with airlift units in delivering supplies to inaccessible areas. Finally, it is meant to show that armed humanitarian intervention against the interests and will of some of the combatants will usually be less sustainable than the alternatives and therefore less useful over the long term to those who need help.

Domestic and Foreign-Policy Consequences

But what if it is clear that serious human rights violations can only be averted by large-scale military action, that reliable cease-fire commitments cannot be obtained, and that the states contributing to a UN force are prepared to accept the casualties and the consequences of failure? Here one must distinguish between state-sponsored crimes against humanity and violence among competing factions within a collapsing state. In some ways the unorganized violence is harder to handle because of the difficulty of bringing political and military pressure to bear on multiple parties.

Public support for the Somalia intervention was not a real problem until late in the crisis. In the United States, public opinion surveys conducted during the crisis suggest a greater acceptance of the intervention than is generally supposed. Polls taken in 1993 and 1994 showed strong support for the U.S. leadership role in UNITAF and considerable patience in the face of casualties. In March 1993, for example, after the first clashes with Aideed's forces and the initial U.S. losses, "84 percent of Americans approved . . . of the use of U.S. forces for humanitarian purposes."[50] Even after the fateful battle between U.S. Army Rangers and Aideed gunmen on October 3, 1993—and the heartrending television pictures of the violation of a soldier's body—Americans supported the Somalia intervention in principle. Sixty-two percent of those surveyed in December 1993 said that "the United States did the 'right thing' to send troops to Somalia to 'make sure shipments of food got through.'"[51]

This approval did not extend to continued U.S. military involvement. Another poll in late 1993 found that "69 percent of people surveyed called for withdrawal of American troops."[52] The Somalia experience suggests that most Americans will support the use of force for humanitarian purposes so long as the purposes and risks are made clear—not only at the outset of an operation (which was done when UNITAF was launched) but throughout its course as the risks and objectives change (which was not done adequately).

For most people, humanitarian intervention raises conflicting moral considerations. The impulse to hold out a helping hand can conflict with the obligation not to place the lives of U.S. troops at risk unnecessarily. Americans do not want to be the world's policemen, but neither do they want their government to ignore the suffering of innocent people. "The challenge," in the words of Admiral Jonathan T. Howe, the U.S. commander of UNOSOM II, "is to find the right boundary line between unwanted interference in the internal affairs of a country and decisive action to prevent crimes against humanity."[53]

The U.S. losses and early departure from Somalia in March 1994 had serious repercussions on domestic politics and foreign policy. At home, many Americans came to believe that "whether or not it succeeded in relieving some of Somalia's misery, the intervention was a foreign policy disaster for the United States."[54] Abroad, the withdrawal of the U.S. units before the job was finished was seen as an abdication of leadership: It was said at the United Nations that U.S. policy toward peacekeeping could be summed up as "not one soldier, not one cent."[55]

This shift from enthusiastic multilateralism to near isolationism led to U.S. opposition to the use of force in places where it might have been effective, at least for limited purposes. In Rwanda, "the first victim of the post-Somalia backlash," and later in Burundi, state-supported genocide was left unchallenged because of U.S. opposition to significant action in the Security Council.[56] And in Bosnia, the United States opposed the use of force to stop ethnic cleansing for several years, even though most of the human rights violations were the result of Serbian aggression against the independent state of Bosnia.[57]

The Somalia experience continues to play a part in the debate on how to respond to the run of civil wars that ravage the poorest nations of the world. These are the "teacup wars . . . the wars of national debilitation" that have emerged as "the new core problem in post–Cold War politics."[58] Why do these devastating ethnic and factional wars, which have so little bearing on the global power situation, raise such hard questions for the major powers? In the United States the answer is that the same bedrock issues are involved as those that have informed the U.S. debate on the uses of force for more than two hundred years.

Among these issues are the long-standing dichotomies in U.S. political attitudes that were discussed in Chapter 4. There is first the unresolved tension between liberal internationalism and isolationism, nowhere more clearly demonstrated than in the national debate over the appropriate uses of U.S. power in the post–Cold War era. The mishaps in Somalia revived the long-standing distrust of UN military action among conservatives. Yet the incident that most angered Americans and turned them against the UN operation—the helicopter raid on Aideed's forces with its ninety-six dead and wounded U.S. soldiers—did not fail because of UN ineffectiveness but because of overlapping chains of command in the assorted U.S. forces that served in UNOSOM II.[59]

Another set of issues that bears on U.S. policy and public opinion toward violent local conflicts concerns the right of intervention in cases of grave violations of the human rights principles established by the UN Charter and the Declaration of Human Rights. The human rights debate is in turn tied to the peculiarly American argument between "idealists" and "realists." Now, as throughout American history, the discussion is between those who believe that the purpose of U.S. policy should be to spread democracy and oppose abuses of power and those who contend that force should be used only in the furtherance of demonstrable strategic interests.[60]

The Ambiguities of "Peace Enforcement"

Since UNOSOM II is commonly referred to as a "peace enforcement" operation, it is worth asking what precisely that term means. Is peace enforcement synonymous with action taken under Chapter VII? Or is it simply a muscular variety of peacekeeping with less-restrictive rules of engagement than the lightly armed, interpositionary peacekeeping missions of the Cold War? Does the term suggest an absence of full consent, or does it encompass missions that have been formally accepted by the parties (as in the UN-authorized NATO operation in the Balkans)? Does it imply particular direction and command responsibilities? And what is the connection between peace enforcement actions that are authorized under Chapter VII and the actual provisions of that chapter, which relate to the mechanisms of collective security rather than the conduct of peacekeeping?

The fact is that the term "peace enforcement" is commonly used without precision, rather like "collective security" and "balance of power" but without the rigorous theory on which those systems are founded. It has a "Don't tread on me!" ring to it, implying vigorous retaliation if the force is attacked. The term also means different things to different governments. British usage is similar to "ad hoc collective security" in the U.S. lexicon, covering UN enforcement actions that the Security Council authorizes but that operate under direction and command arrangements outside the machinery of Chapter VII. France, on the other hand, uses the term to denote a new category of UN operation that requires the use of force but is not directed against an act of aggression.[61]

China has a singular position on the meaning of "peace enforcement" and the citation of Chapter VII in authorizing resolutions. It is, briefly, that peacekeeping operations, including those to which all of the parties agree, should be established under the provisions of Chapter VII. For example, the 1998 UN election-monitoring mission in the Central African Republic (MINURCA) was authorized under Chapter VII at China's initiative. This was despite the fact that the parties had not only given their consent to the mission but had already been disarmed by France in an earlier unilateral operation of its own. The somewhat circuitous point that China is making is that Chapter VII applies not only to enforcement action against aggression but also to traditional consensual peacekeeping: Therefore, by inference, Chapter VII does *not* apply to armed "peace enforcement" action in conflicts within states, which China strongly opposes. One may agree generally with China's opposition to UN intervention in domestic conflicts while believing that no purpose is served by authorizing peacekeeping missions under Chapter VII. In fact, the effect is to obscure the crucial differences between peacekeeping and enforcement actions in the use of force and, in doing so, to risk resorting to the armed intervention in civil wars that China opposes.

To return to Somalia, the citation of Chapter VII in the authorizing resolutions of UNITAF and UNOSOM II served as a warning that armed opposition would be suppressed with whatever force was required. More formally, the reference to Chapter VII meant that the Security Council, acting under Article 39, had determined "the existence of [a] threat to the peace [or] breach of the peace" and was taking action under Article 42 "to maintain or restore international peace and security." This was the sense of the reference to Chapter VII in the UNITAF and UNOSOM II resolutions. And yet it is clear that in Somalia the violence was internal, the threat to international peace was minimal, and the motivation for the intervention was humanitarian.

The problem with this new category is not so much that Article 2, paragraph 7 is sometimes circumvented or that the terms "peace enforcement" and "Chapter VII" are sometimes used loosely. Rather, it is that these two terms, used together, blur the distinction between peacekeeping and collective security. They contribute to the soothing impression that full consent may not be necessary in a particular UN action since, by definition, "enforcement" under Chapter VII operates without unanimous consent. And the failure to distinguish clearly between enforcement and consensual action can—and in Somalia did—lead to unworkable direction-and-command arrangements.

It does not follow that powerful peacekeeping operations with mandates providing for strong retaliation must be avoided. As the NATO operation in the Balkans has shown, such missions can achieve their military objectives so long as the parties accept their mandates and rules of engagement. In other words, the level of force does not define the nature of the intervention. Separation-of-parties actions are peacekeeping rather than collective security, no matter how strong the UN forces are on the ground and in reserve, and peacekeeping requires the unqualified consent of the parties. The difficulty is that reliable commitments of consent are hard to come by in intercommunal conflicts. No one knows the difficulties better than the Red Cross. "In today's conflicts," observes ICRC Director General Peter Fuchs, "there may be five, six, seven parties, a lot of militias, bandits and self-named warlords. No one is in control."[62]

There is nothing new about the necessity for the parties to an internal conflict to agree among themselves on the need for outside help in carrying out a cease-fire agreement. Regional peacekeeping operations in Lebanon in 1983–1984 and more recently in Liberia came to grief because some of the competing factions opposed them. The absence of full consent led to assaults against the peacekeepers and, inevitably, to the hard choice of escalating the violence or appearing indecisive. The same dynamic operated in Somalia. It was a small step from retaliating against General Aideed for his attacks on UN troops to calling him the enemy— and from there to participation in the Somali civil war.

The ambiguities of "peace enforcement" also led to command-and-control problems after UNOSOM II replaced UNITAF. Most troubling from the standpoint of the force commander, Lieutenant General Cevit Bir of Turkey, was the lack of clear guidance as to who had the authority to order the use of force in situations other than self-defense. One reason for the ambiguity was the difficulty of anticipating the challenges that UNOSOM II was likely to face and of defining rules of engagement to cover them all. As it turned out, the challenges ranged from sallies by armed adolescents to organized attacks by units armed with heavy weapons: Each response had to be made on an ad hoc basis and, what was even harder for UN headquarters, with great speed.

Another problem in nonconsensual "peace enforcement" actions, and in UNOSOM II in particular, is the need to disarm the belligerents if the accomplishments of a UN operation are to survive its departure. The principal U.S. military review of the Somalia operations observes that "forcible disarmament is the 'bright line' of peace operations: when you cross it, you have entered a de facto state of war."[63] And in that case the operation is neither peacekeeping nor peace enforcement. It is armed enforcement action, which to succeed must be controlled by the Security Council, directed by the permanent members in accordance with the charter, and commanded by the principal contributing state.

The most coherent definition of peace enforcement is contained in Secretary General Boutros-Ghali's January 1992 report to the Security Council, published as "An Agenda for Peace." There the term is used to denote a category of collective force lying between the self-defense guidelines of peacekeeping and the war powers of collective security. With Somalia in mind, the secretary general recommends that the Security Council consider the utilization of "peace-enforcement units" to restore the peace in cases where cease-fires have been agreed to but not complied with. If these situations fall short of aggression, he argues, they nevertheless require heavier arms and more extensive training than traditional peacekeeping missions.

In the "Agenda for Peace" scheme, these peace-enforcement units would be ready for duty on the call of the Security Council. Although authorized and controlled by the Security Council, they "would, as in the case of peace-keeping forces, be under the command of the Secretary-General."[64] After the withdrawal from Somalia, Boutros-Ghali retracted the idea that the secretary general should command UN combat forces. However, as recounted in the next chapter, elements of the proposal reappear in other efforts to deal with the need for faster response time and adequate armed forces to respond to situations that are spinning out of control like those in Somalia and Bosnia.

In a January 1995 supplement to "An Agenda for Peace," Boutros-Ghali wrote that "neither the Security Council nor the Secretary-General at present has the capacity to deploy, direct, command and control operations [for the purposes of Chapter VII.]"[65] Two years later, Kofi Annan continued to reflect this more modest vision of the secretary general's peace-and-security functions in his statement accepting the office of secretary general.[66]

In considering the uses of armed humanitarian intervention, a distinction must be made between indiscriminate civil violence in a collapsing state, as in Somalia, and state-sponsored human rights violations against minority groups. State-inspired violations that are so grave in the eyes of the international community as to require the use of force against an unwilling government cannot be dealt with by peacekeeping or peace enforcement. Where genocide or ethnic cleansing threatens, the same capabilities are required as those needed to defeat cross-border aggression. High on the list is the capacity to deploy elements of a task force of concerned states with great speed. To do this, the Security Council needs to have standby forces available to it that can be dispatched before the coercion becomes too widespread to be stopped. An international deterrent force, although intended primarily to prevent aggression, could provide this capacity in crimes against humanity that the Security Council decided to prevent or suppress with force.

10

Problems on the Path to an
International Deterrent System

Any study of collective security's applicability to the security problems of the twenty-first century must deal not only with the merits of the system but with the process of getting there. The first question is whether to proceed incrementally, extending the scope of peacekeeping to cover the more effective use of force in local conflicts, or to try to move directly to a modified collective-security system based on the UN Charter. The answer turns partly on a judgment as to whether the resources and the political will exist for a financially sound and militarily credible international deterrent force.

The resource situation is not reassuring. The United Nations has neither the money to pay for large new conventional peacekeeping operations, the troops to carry them out, nor the headquarters people to run them. For emergency operations requiring the rapid deployment of armed power, it has virtually no infrastructure at all. And there is not much hope on the horizon. The overall UN debt, as of August 31, 1998, came to $2.68 billion, of which $1. 6 billion was owed by the United States. These and earlier shortfalls have translated into delayed contingent arrivals in Namibia, insufficient troops and inferior arms in the early stages of the Somalia crisis, and an inability to take serious action in Rwanda.

It is fair to ask if there would be greater financial support for an international deterrent force. Although less expensive than the armed forces contemplated in the UN Charter, an IDF is not cost free. For the advanced military powers, the expenses would include the training of small, mobile contingents for the states that cannot afford them; the provision of modern weapons, logistics facilities, and communications equipment to the poorer countries; and the contribution of air transport in regional rapid-deployment maneuvers.

The creation of an international deterrent force would also have political costs. In the United States, any movement toward a UN force is politically charged, even if the purpose is deterrence and the basic function is
burden-sharing. The sensitivity stems from perceived limitations of sovereignty and from hostility among conservatives in Congress to the
United Nations as an institution. But there is another side to the story.
Over the years, numerous surveys of American public opinion have
shown that a sizable majority of the people support the United Nations
and the leadership that the United States has exercised in it through most
of its history. Even in the most trying situations, like Korea and Somalia,
popular support has been broad and enduring so long as the purposes
and risks of U.S. involvement have been made clear.

In late 1998, the most urgent UN problem for the United States is not
an outdated security system but the imminent loss of the U.S. vote in the
General Assembly. This is almost certain to happen if Congress does not
appropriate money for U.S. arrears by the end of the year. Article 19 of
the UN Charter provides for automatic suspension of voting rights when
a member's debt equals or exceeds the amount of the contributions due
from it for the preceding two years. There is, of course, no question of
movement toward a more effective security system until the United
States has paid a significant portion of its arrears.

In considering the steps to an updated security system, it may be useful to compare briefly the IDF concept with a proposal that has been the
starting point for recent discussions of the UN's role in the post-Soviet
world. This is a proposal by former UN Under Secretary General Sir
Brian Urquhart for a volunteer military force capable of armed intervention in violent local conflicts.[1] Urquhart argues that "a five-thousand-
strong light infantry force [costing] about $380 million a year to train and
equip" could give the Security Council the capacity to deploy credible
and effective peace enforcement units at an early stage in local insurgen-
cies. The purpose would be "to impose the Security Council's decisions
on partisan militias and other nongovernmental groups . . . in chaotic or
violent situations within states or former states."[2]

Urquhart's proposal and the IDF concept involve different paths to implementation as well as different kinds of conflicts. The volunteer-force
plan reflects an incremental approach. It is a stage on the way to activat-
ing the provisions of Chapter VII, when and if that becomes possible. A
deterrent force, on the other hand, is designed to deal with aggression
and other threats to international security that cannot be managed by
more forceful peacekeeping. It necessarily involves an effort to move directly to a modified collective-security system through the negotiation of
Article 43 agreements.

In the end, there is only one way to find out if a UN Charter-based deterrent system is affordable, militarily feasible, and politically acceptable, and that is for the permanent members to put concrete proposals to the membership. Not until governments focus at the highest levels on these issues—and each analyzes the costs and benefits in its particular case—can anyone predict whether an international deterrent force could provide the basis of a security system for the twenty-first century. Problems of scarce financial and military resources might turn out to be conclusive. On the other hand, the members might decide that an effective system of war prevention was cheaper than the alternative.

Appendix: The Charter of the United Nations

Introductory Note

The Charter of the United Nations was signed on 26 June 1945, in San Francisco, at the conclusion of the United Nations Conference on International Organization, and came into force on 24 October 1945. The Statute of the International Court of Justice is an integral part of the Charter.

Amendments to Articles 23, 27, and 61 of the Charter were adopted by the General Assembly on 17 December 1963 and came into force on 31 August 1965. A further amendment to Article 61 was adopted by the General Assembly on 20 December 1971 and came into force on 24 September 1973. An amendment to Article 109, adopted by the General Assembly on 20 December 1965, came into force on 12 June 1968.

The amendment to Article 23 enlarges the membership of the Security Council from eleven to fifteen. The amended Article 27 provides that decisions of the Security Council on procedural matters shall be made by an affirmative vote of nine members (formerly seven) and on all other matters by an affirmative vote of nine members (formerly seven), including the concurring votes of the five permanent members of the Security Council.

The amendment to Article 61, which entered into force on 31 August 1965, enlarged the membership of the Economic and Social Council from eighteen to twenty-seven. The subsequent amendment to that Article, which entered into force on 24 September 1973, further increased the membership of the Council from twenty-seven to fifty-four.

The amendment to Article 109, which relates to the first paragraph of that Article, provides that a General Conference of Member States for the purpose of reviewing the Charter may be held at a date and place to be fixed by a two-thirds vote of the members of the General Assembly and by a vote of any nine members (formerly seven) of the Security Council. Paragraph 3 of Article 109, which deals with the consideration of a possible review conference during the tenth regular session of the General Assembly, has been retained in its original form in its reference to a "vote, of any seven members of the Security Council," the paragraph having been acted upon in 1955 by the General Assembly, at its tenth regular session, and by the Security Council.

Charter of the United Nations

WE THE PEOPLES OF THE UNITED NATIONS DETERMINED

to save succeeding generations from the scourge of war, which twice in our lifetime has brought untold sorrow to mankind, and

to reaffirm faith in fundamental human rights, in the dignity and worth of the human person, in the equal rights of men and women and of nations large and small, and

to establish conditions under which justice and respect for the obligations arising from treaties and other sources of international law can be maintained, and

to promote social progress and better standards of life in larger freedom,

AND FOR THESE ENDS

to practice tolerance and live together in peace with one another as good neighbours, and

to unite our strength to maintain international peace and security, and

to ensure, by the acceptance of principles and the institution of methods, that armed force shall not be used, save in the common interest, and

to employ international machinery for the promotion of the economic and social advancement of all peoples,

HAVE RESOLVED TO COMBINE OUR EFFORTS TO ACCOMPLISH THESE AIMS

Accordingly, our respective Governments, through representatives assembled in the city of San Francisco, who have exhibited their full powers found to be in good and due form, have agreed to the present Charter of the United Nations and do hereby establish an international organization to be known as the United Nations.

Chapter I
Purposes and Principles

Article 1.

The Purposes of the United Nations are:

1. To maintain international peace and security, and to that end: to take effective collective measures for the prevention and removal of threats to the peace, and for the suppression of acts of aggression or other breaches of the peace, and to bring about by peaceful means, and in conformity with the principles of justice and international law, adjustment or settlement of international disputes or situations which might lead to a breach of the peace;
2. To develop friendly relations among nations based on respect for the principle of equal rights and self-determination of peoples, and to take other appropriate measures to strengthen universal peace;
3. To achieve international co-operation in solving international problems of an economic, social, cultural, or humanitarian character, and in promoting and encouraging respect for human rights and for fundamental freedoms for all without distinction as to race, sex, language, or religion; and

4. To be a centre for harmonizing the actions of nations in the attainment of these common ends.

Article 2.

The Organization and its Members, in pursuit of the Purposes stated in Article 1, shall act in accordance with the following Principles.

1. The Organization is based on the principle of the sovereign equality of all its Members.
2. All Members, in order to ensure to all of them the rights and benefits resulting from membership, shall fulfill in good faith the obligations assumed by them in accordance with the present Charter.
3. All Members shall settle their international disputes by peaceful means in such a manner that international peace and security, and justice, are not endangered.
4. All Members shall refrain in their international relations from the threat or use of force against the territorial integrity or political independence of any state, or in any other manner inconsistent with the Purposes of the United Nations.
5. All Members shall give the United Nations every assistance in any action it takes in accordance with the present Charter, and shall refrain from giving assistance to any state against which the United Nations is taking preventive or enforcement action.
6. The Organization shall ensure that states which are not Members of the United Nations act in accordance with these Principles so far as may be necessary for the maintenance of international peace and security.
7. Nothing contained in the present Charter shall authorize the United Nations to intervene in matters which are essentially within the domestic jurisdiction of any state or shall require the Members to submit such matters to settlement under the present Charter; but this principle shall not prejudice the application of enforcement measures under Chapter VII.

Chapter II
Membership

Article 3.

The original Members of the United Nations shall be the states which, having participated in the United Nations Conference on International Organization at San Francisco, or having previously signed the Declaration by United Nations of 1 January 1942, sign the present Charter and ratify it in accordance with Article 110.

Article 4.

1. Membership in the United Nations is open to all other peace-loving states which accept the obligations contained in the present Charter

and, in the judgment of the Organization, are able and willing to carry out these obligations.

2. The admission of any such state to membership in the United Nations will be effected by a decision of the General Assembly upon the recommendation of the Security Council.

Article 5.

A Member of the United Nations against which preventive or enforcement action has been taken by the Security Council may be suspended from the exercise of the rights and privileges of membership by the General Assembly upon the recommendation of the Security Council. The exercise of these rights and privileges may be restored by the Security Council.

Article 6.

A Member of the United Nations which has persistently violated the Principles contained in the present Charter may be expelled from the Organization by the General Assembly upon the recommendation of the Security Council.

Chapter III
Organs

Article 7.

1. There are established as the principal organs of the United Nations: a General Assembly, a Security Council, an Economic and Social Council, a Trusteeship Council, an International Court of Justice, and a Secretariat.
2. Such subsidiary organs as may be found necessary may be established in accordance with the present Charter.

Article 8.

The United Nations shall place no restrictions on the eligibility of men and women to participate in any capacity and under conditions of equality in its principal and subsidiary organs.

Chapter IV
The General Assembly

Composition

Article 9.

1. The General Assembly shall consist of all the Members of the United Nations.
2. Each Member shall have not more than five representatives in the General Assembly.

Functions and Powers

Article 10.

The General Assembly may discuss any questions or any matters within the scope of the present Charter or relating to the powers and functions of any organs provided for in the present Charter, and, except as provided in Article 12, may make recommendations to the Members of the United Nations or to the Security Council or to both on any such questions or matters.

Article 11.

1. The General Assembly may consider the general principles of co-operation in the maintenance of international peace and security, including the principles governing disarmament and the regulation of armaments, and may make recommendations with regard to such principles to the Members or to the Security Council or to both.
2. The General Assembly may discuss any questions relating to the maintenance of international peace and security brought before it by any Member of the United Nations, or by the Security Council, or by a state which is not a Member of the United Nations in accordance with Article 35, paragraph 2, and, except as provided in Article 12, may make recommendations with regard to any such questions to the state or states concerned or to the Security Council or to both. Any such question on which action is necessary shall be referred to the Security Council by the General Assembly either before or after discussion.
3. The General Assembly may call the attention of the Security Council to situations which are likely to endanger international peace and security.
4. The powers of the General Assembly set forth in this Article shall not limit the general scope of Article 10.

Article 12.

1. While the Security Council is exercising in respect of any dispute or situation the functions assigned to it in the present Charter, the General Assembly shall not make any recommendation with regard to that dispute or situation unless the Security Council so requests.
2. The Secretary-General, with the consent of the Security Council, shall notify the General Assembly at each session of any matters relative to the maintenance of international peace and security which are being dealt with by the Security Council and shall similarly notify the General Assembly, or the Members of the United Nations if the General Assembly is not in session, immediately the Security Council ceases to deal with such matters.

Article 13.

1. The General Assembly shall initiate studies and make recommendations for the purpose of:

    A.   promoting international co-operation in the political field and encouraging the progressive development of international law and its codification;

    B.   promoting international co-operation in the economic, social, cultural, educational, and health fields, and assisting in the realization of human rights and fundamental freedoms for all without distinction as to race, sex, language, or religion.

2. The further responsibilities, functions and powers of the General Assembly with respect to matters mentioned in paragraph 1 (b) above are set forth in Chapters IX and X.

Article 14.

Subject to the provisions of Article 12, the General Assembly may recommend measures for the peaceful adjustment of any situation, regardless of origin, which it deems likely to impair the general welfare or friendly relations among nations, including situations resulting from a violation of the provisions of the present Charter setting forth the Purposes and Principles of the United Nations.

Article 15.

1. The General Assembly shall receive and consider annual and special reports from the Security Council; these reports shall include an account of the measures that the Security Council has decided upon or taken to maintain international peace and security.

2. The General Assembly shall receive and consider reports from the other organs of the United Nations.

Article 16.

The General Assembly shall perform such functions with respect to the international trusteeship system as are assigned to it under Chapters XII and XIII, including the approval of the trusteeship agreements for areas not designated as strategic.

Article 17.

1. The General Assembly shall consider and approve the budget of the Organization.

2. The expenses of the Organization shall be borne by the Members as apportioned by the General Assembly.

3. The General Assembly shall consider and approve any financial and budgetary arrangements with specialized agencies referred to in Article 57 and shall examine the administrative budgets of such specialized agencies with a view to making recommendations to the agencies concerned.

Voting

Article 18.

1. Each member of the General Assembly shall have one vote.
2. Decisions of the General Assembly on important questions shall be made by a two-thirds majority of the members present and voting. These questions shall include: recommendations with respect to the maintenance of international peace and security, the election of the non-permanent members of the Security Council, the election of the members of the Economic and Social Council, the election of members of the Trusteeship Council in accordance with paragraph 1 (c) of Article 86, the admission of new Members to the United Nations, the suspension of the rights and privileges of membership, the expulsion of Members, questions relating to the operation of the trusteeship system, and budgetary questions.
3. Decisions on other questions, including the determination of additional categories of questions to be decided by a two-thirds majority, shall be made by a majority of the members present and voting.

Article 19.

A Member of the United Nations which is in arrears in the payment of its financial contributions to the Organization shall have no vote in the General Assembly if the amount of its arrears equals or exceeds the amount of the contributions due from it for the preceding two full years. The General Assembly may, nevertheless, permit such a Member to vote if it is satisfied that the failure to pay is due to conditions beyond the control of the Member.

Procedure

Article 20.

The General Assembly shall meet in regular annual sessions and in such special sessions as occasion may require. Special sessions shall be convoked by the Secretary-General at the request of the Security Council or of a majority of the Members of the United Nations.

Article 21.

The General Assembly shall adopt its own rules of procedure. It shall elect its President for each session.

Article 22.

The General Assembly may establish such subsidiary organs as it deems necessary for the performance of its functions.

Chapter V
The Security Council

Composition

Article 23.

1. The Security Council shall consist of fifteen Members of the United Nations. The Republic of China, France, the Union of Soviet Socialist Republics, the United Kingdom of Great Britain and Northern Ireland, and the United States of America shall be permanent members of the Security Council. The General Assembly shall elect ten other Members of the United Nations to be non-permanent members of the Security Council, due regard being specially paid, in the first instance to the contribution of Members of the United Nations to the maintenance of international peace and security and to the other purposes of the Organization, and also to equitable geographical distribution.
2. The non-permanent members of the Security Council shall be elected for a term of two years. In the first election of the non-permanent members after the increase of the membership of the Security Council from eleven to fifteen, two of the four additional members shall be chosen for a term of one year. A retiring member shall not be eligible for immediate re-election.
3. Each member of the Security Council shall have one representative.

Functions and Powers

Article 24.

1. In order to ensure prompt and effective action by the United Nations, its Members confer on the Security Council primary responsibility for the maintenance of international peace and security, and agree that in carrying out its duties under this responsibility the Security Council acts on their behalf.
2. In discharging these duties the Security Council shall act in accordance with the Purposes and Principles of the United Nations. The specific powers granted to the Security Council for the discharge of these duties are laid down in Chapters VI, VII, VIII, and XII.
3. The Security Council shall submit annual and, when necessary, special reports to the General Assembly for its consideration.

Article 25.

The Members of the United Nations agree to accept and carry out the decisions of the Security Council in accordance with the present Charter.

Article 26.

In order to promote the establishment and maintenance of international peace and security with the least diversion for armaments of the world's human and economic resources, the Security Council shall be responsible for formulating, with the assistance of the Military Staff Committee referred to in Article 47, plans to be submitted to the Members of the United Nations for the establishment of a system for the regulation of armaments.

Voting

Article 27.

1. Each member of the Security Council shall have one vote.
2. Decisions of the Security Council on procedural matters shall be made by an affirmative vote of nine members.
3. Decisions of the Security Council on all other matters shall be made by an affirmative vote of nine members including the concurring votes of the permanent members; provided that, in decisions under Chapter VI, and under paragraph 3 of Article 52, a party to a dispute shall abstain from voting.

Procedure

Article 28.

1. The Security Council shall be so organized as to be able to function continuously. Each member of the Security Council shall for this purpose be represented at all times at the seat of the Organization.
2. The Security Council shall hold periodic meetings at which each of its members may, if it so desires, be represented by a member of the government or by some other specially designated representative.
3. The Security Council may hold meetings at such places other than the seat of the Organization as in its judgment will best facilitate its work.

Article 29.

The Security Council may establish such subsidiary organs as it deems necessary for the performance of its functions.

Article 30.

The Security Council shall adopt its own rules of procedure, including the method of selecting its President.

Article 31.

Any Member of the United Nations which is not a member of the Security Council may participate, without vote, in the discussion of any question brought before the Security Council whenever the latter considers that the interests of that Member are specially affected.

Article 32.

Any Member of the United Nations which is not a member of the Security Council or any state which is not a Member of the United Nations, if it is a party to a dispute under consideration by the Security Council, shall be invited to participate, without vote, in the discussion relating to the dispute. The Security Council shall lay down such conditions as it deems just for the participation of a state which is not a Member of the United Nations.

Chapter VI
Pacific Settlement of Disputes

Article 33.

1. The parties to any dispute, the continuance of which is likely to endanger the maintenance of international peace and security, shall, first of all, seek a solution by negotiation, enquiry, mediation, conciliation, arbitration, judicial settlement, resort to regional agencies or arrangements, or other peaceful means of their own choice.
2. The Security Council shall, when it deems necessary, call upon the parties to settle their dispute by such means.

Article 34.

The Security Council may investigate any dispute, or any situation which might lead to international friction or give rise to a dispute, in order to determine whether the continuance of the dispute or situation is likely to endanger the maintenance of international peace and security.

Article 35.

1. Any Member of the United Nations may bring any dispute, or any situation of the nature referred to in Article 34, to the attention of the Security Council or of the General Assembly.
2. A state which is not a Member of the United Nations may bring to the attention of the Security Council or of the General Assembly any dispute to which it is a party if it accepts in advance, for the purposes of the dispute, the obligations of pacific settlement provided in the present Charter.
3. The proceedings of the General Assembly in respect of matters brought to its attention under this Article will be subject to the provisions of Articles 11 and 12.

Article 36.

1. The Security Council may, at any stage of a dispute of the nature referred to in Article 33 or of a situation of like nature, recommend appropriate procedures or methods of adjustment.

2. The Security Council should take into consideration any procedures for the settlement of the dispute which have already been adopted by the parties.
3. In making recommendations under this Article the Security Council should also take into consideration that legal disputes should as a general rule be referred by the parties to the International Court of Justice in accordance with the provisions of the Statute of the Court.

Article 37.

1. Should the parties to a dispute of the nature referred to in Article 33 fail to settle it by the means indicated in that Article, they shall refer it to the Security Council.
2. If the Security Council deems that the continuance of the dispute is in fact likely to endanger the maintenance of international peace and security, it shall decide whether to take action under Article 36 or to recommend such terms of settlement as it may consider appropriate.

Article 38.

Without prejudice to the provisions of Articles 33 to 37, the Security Council may, if all the parties to any dispute so request, make recommendations to the parties with a view to a pacific settlement of the dispute.

Chapter VII
Action with Respect to Threats to the Peace, Breaches of the Peace, and Acts of Aggression

Article 39.

The Security Council shall determine the existence of any threat to the peace, breach of the peace, or act of aggression and shall make recommendations, or decide what measures shall be taken in accordance with Articles 41 and 42, to maintain or restore international peace and security.

Article 40.

In order to prevent an aggravation of the situation, the Security Council may, before making the recommendations or deciding upon the measures provided for in Article 39, call upon the parties concerned to comply with such provisional measures as it deems necessary or desirable. Such provisional measures shall be without prejudice to the rights, claims, or position of the parties concerned. The Security Council shall duly take account of failure to comply with such provisional measures.

Article 41.

The Security Council may decide what measures not involving the use of armed force are to be employed to give effect to its decisions, and it may call upon the Members of the United Nations to apply such measures. These may include complete or partial interruption of economic relations and of rail, sea, air, postal, telegraphic, radio, and other means of communication, and the severance of diplomatic relations.

Article 42.

Should the Security Council consider that measures provided for in Article 41 would be inadequate or have proved to be inadequate, it may take such action by air, sea, or land forces as may be necessary to maintain or restore international peace and security. Such action may include demonstrations, blockade, and other operations by air, sea, or land forces of Members of the United Nations.

Article 43.

1. All Members of the United Nations, in order to contribute to the maintenance of international peace and security, undertake to make available to the Security Council, on its call and in accordance with a special agreement or agreements, armed forces, assistance, and facilities, including rights of passage, necessary for the purpose of maintaining international peace and security.
2. Such agreement or agreements shall govern the numbers and types of forces, their degree of readiness and general location, and the nature of the facilities and assistance to be provided.
3. The agreement or agreements shall be negotiated as soon as possible on the initiative of the Security Council. They shall be concluded between the Security Council and Members or between the Security Council and groups of Members and shall be subject to ratification by the signatory states in accordance with their respective constitutional processes.

Article 44.

When the Security Council has decided to use force it shall, before calling upon a Member not represented on it to provide armed forces in fulfilment of the obligations assumed under Article 43, invite that Member, if the Member so desires, to participate in the decisions of the Security Council concerning the employment of contingents of that Member's armed forces.

Article 45.

In order to enable the United Nations to take urgent military measures, Members shall hold immediately available national air-force contingents for combined international enforcement action. The strength and degree of readiness of these contingents and plans for their combined action shall be determined within the limits laid down in the special agreement or agreements referred to in Article 43, by the Security Council with the assistance of the Military Staff Committee.

Article 46.

Plans for the application of armed force shall be made by the Security Council with the assistance of the Military Staff Committee.

Article 47.

1. There shall be established a Military Staff Committee to advise and assist the Security Council on all questions relating to the Security Council's military requirements for the maintenance of international peace and security, the employment and command of forces placed at its disposal, the regulation of armaments, and possible disarmament.
2. The Military Staff Committee shall consist of the Chiefs of Staff of the permanent members of the Security Council or their representatives. Any Member of the United Nations not permanently represented on the Committee shall be invited by the Committee to be associated with it when the efficient discharge of the Committee's responsibilities requires the participation of that Member in its work.
3. The Military Staff Committee shall be responsible under the Security Council for the strategic direction of any armed forces placed at the disposal of the Security Council. Questions relating to the command of such forces shall be worked out subsequently.
4. The Military Staff Committee, with the authorization of the Security Council and after consultation with appropriate regional agencies, may establish regional sub-committees.

Article 48.

1. The action required to carry out the decisions of the Security Council for the maintenance of international peace and security shall be taken by all the Members of the United Nations or by some of them, as the Security Council may determine.
2. Such decisions shall be carried out by the Members of the United Nations directly and through their action in the appropriate international agencies of which they are members.

Article 49.

The Members of the United Nations shall join in affording mutual assistance in carrying out the measures decided upon by the Security Council.

Article 50.

If preventive or enforcement measures against any state are taken by the Security Council, any other state, whether a Member of the United Nations or not, which finds itself confronted with special economic problems arising from the carrying out of those measures shall have the right to consult the Security Council with regard to a solution of those problems.

Article 51.

Nothing in the present Charter shall impair the inherent right of individual or collective self-defence if an armed attack occurs against a Member of the United Nations, until the Security Council has taken measures necessary to maintain international peace and security. Measures taken by Members in the exercise of this right of self-defence shall be immediately reported to the Security Council and shall not in any way affect the authority and responsibility of the Security Council under the present Charter to take at any time such action as it deems necessary in order to maintain or restore international peace and security.

Chapter VIII
Regional Arrangements

Article 52.

1. Nothing in the present Charter precludes the existence of regional arrangements or agencies for dealing with such matters relating to the maintenance of international peace and security as are appropriate for regional action provided that such arrangements or agencies and their activities are consistent with the Purposes and Principles of the United Nations.
2. The Members of the United Nations entering into such arrangements or constituting such agencies shall make every effort to achieve pacific settlement of local disputes through such regional arrangements or by such regional agencies before referring them to the Security Council.
3. The Security Council shall encourage the development of pacific settlement of local disputes through such regional arrangements or by such regional agencies either on the initiative of the states concerned or by reference from the Security Council.
4. This Article in no way impairs the application of Articles 34 and 35.

Article 53.

1. The Security Council shall, where appropriate, utilize such regional arrangements or agencies for enforcement action under its authority. But no enforcement action shall be taken under regional arrangements or by regional agencies without the authorization of the Security Council, with the exception of measures against any enemy state, as defined in paragraph 2 of this Article, provided for pursuant to Article 107 or in regional arrangements directed against renewal of aggressive policy on the part of any such state, until such time as the Organization

may, on request of the Governments concerned, be charged with the responsibility for preventing further aggression by such a state.

2. The term enemy state as used in paragraph 1 of this Article applies to any state which during the Second World War has been an enemy of any signatory of the present Charter.

Article 54.

The Security Council shall at all times be kept fully informed of activities undertaken or in contemplation under regional arrangements or by regional agencies for the maintenance of international peace and security.

Chapter IX
International Economic and Social Co-operation

Article 55.

With a view to the creation of conditions of stability and well-being which are necessary for peaceful and friendly relations among nations based on respect for the principle of equal rights and self-determination of peoples, the United Nations shall promote:

A. higher standards of living, full employment, and conditions of economic and social progress and development;
B. solutions of international economic, social, health, and related problems; and international cultural and educational cooperation; and
C. universal respect for, and observance of, human rights and fundamental freedoms for all without distinction as to race, sex, language, or religion.

Article 56.

All Members pledge themselves to take joint and separate action in co-operation with the Organization for the achievement of the purposes set forth in Article 55.

Article 57.

1. The various specialized agencies, established by intergovernmental agreement and having wide international responsibilities, as defined in their basic instruments, in economic, social, cultural, educational, health, and related fields, shall be brought into relationship with the United Nations in accordance with the provisions of Article 63.
2. Such agencies thus brought into relationship with the United Nations are hereinafter referred to as specialized agencies.

Article 58.

The Organization shall make recommendations for the co-ordination of the policies and activities of the specialized agencies.

Article 59.

The Organization shall, where appropriate, initiate negotiations among the states concerned for the creation of any new specialized agencies required for the accomplishment of the purposes set forth in Article 55.

Article 60.

Responsibility for the discharge of the functions of the Organization set forth in this Chapter shall be vested in the General Assembly and, under the authority of the General Assembly, in the Economic and Social Council, which shall have for this purpose the powers set forth in Chapter X.

Chapter X
The Economic and Social Council

Composition

Article 61.

1. The Economic and Social Council shall consist of fifty-four Members of the United Nations elected by the General Assembly.
2. Subject to the provisions of paragraph 3, eighteen members of the Economic and Social Council shall be elected each year for a term of three years. A retiring member shall be eligible for immediate re-election.
3. At the first election after the increase in the membership of the Economic and Social Council from twenty-seven to fifty-four members, in addition to the members elected in place of the nine members whose term of office expires at the end of that year, twenty-seven additional members shall be elected. Of these twenty-seven additional members, the term of office of nine members so elected shall expire at the end of one year, and of nine other members at the end of two years, in accordance with arrangements made by the General Assembly.
4. Each member of the Economic and Social Council shall have one representative.

Functions and Powers

Article 62.

1. The Economic and Social Council may make or initiate studies and reports with respect to international economic, social, cultural, educational, health, and related matters and may make recommendations with respect to any such matters to the General Assembly to the Members of the United Nations, and to the specialized agencies concerned.
2. It may make recommendations for the purpose of promoting respect for, and observance of, human rights and fundamental freedoms for all.

3. It may prepare draft conventions for submission to the General Assembly, with respect to matters falling within its competence.
4. It may call, in accordance with the rules prescribed by the United Nations, international conferences on matters falling within its competence.

Article 63.

1. The Economic and Social Council may enter into agreements with any of the agencies referred to in Article 57, defining the terms on which the agency concerned shall be brought into relationship with the United Nations. Such agreements shall be subject to approval by the General Assembly.
2. It may co-ordinate the activities of the specialized agencies through consultation with and recommendations to such agencies and through recommendations to the General Assembly and to the Members of the United Nations.

Article 64.

1. The Economic and Social Council may take appropriate steps to obtain regular reports from the specialized agencies. It may make arrangements with the Members of the United Nations and with the specialized agencies to obtain reports on the steps taken to give effect to its own recommendations and to recommendations on matters falling within its competence made by the General Assembly.
2. It may communicate its observations on these reports to the General Assembly.

Article 65.

The Economic and Social Council may furnish information to the Security Council and shall assist the Security Council upon its request.

Article 66.

1. The Economic and Social Council shall perform such functions as fall within its competence in connexion with the carrying out of the recommendations of the General Assembly.
2. It may, with the approval of the General Assembly, perform services at the request of Members of the United Nations and at the request of specialized agencies.
3. It shall perform such other functions as are specified elsewhere in the present Charter or as may be assigned to it by the General Assembly.

Voting

Article 67.

1. Each member of the Economic and Social Council shall have one vote.

2. Decisions of the Economic and Social Council shall be made by a majority of the members present and voting.

Procedure

Article 68.

The Economic and Social Council shall set up commissions in economic and social fields and for the promotion of human rights, and such other commissions as may be required for the performance of its functions.

Article 69.

The Economic and Social Council shall invite any Member of the United Nations to participate, without vote, in its deliberations on any matter of particular concern to that Member.

Article 70.

The Economic and Social Council may make arrangements for representatives of the specialized agencies to participate, without vote, in its deliberations and in those of the commissions established by it, and for its representatives to participate in the deliberations of the specialized agencies.

Article 71.

The Economic and Social Council may make suitable arrangements for consultation with non-governmental organizations which are concerned with matters within its competence. Such arrangements may be made with international organizations and, where appropriate, with national organizations after consultation with the Member of the United Nations concerned.

Article 72.

1. The Economic and Social Council shall adopt its own rules of procedure, including the method of selecting its President.
2. The Economic and Social Council shall meet as required in accordance with its rules, which shall include provision for the convening of meetings on the request of a majority of its members.

Chapter XI
Declaration Regarding
Non-Self-Governing Territories

Article 73.

Members of the United Nations which have or assume responsibilities for the administration of territories whose peoples have not yet attained a full measure of self-government recognize the principle that the interests of the inhabitants of these territories are paramount, and accept as a sacred trust the obligation to promote to the utmost, within the system of international peace and security established by the present Charter, the well-being of the inhabitants of these territories, and, to this end:

A. to ensure, with due respect for the culture of the peoples concerned, their political, economic, social, and educational advancement, their just treatment, and their protection against abuses;
B. to develop self-government, to take due account of the political aspirations of the peoples, and to assist them in the progressive development of their free political institutions, according to the particular circumstances of each territory and its peoples and their varying stages of advancement;
C. to further international peace and security;
D. to promote constructive measures of development, to encourage research, and to co-operate with one another and, when and where appropriate, with specialized international bodies with a view to the practical achievement of the social, economic, and scientific purposes set forth in this Article; and
E. to transmit regularly to the Secretary-General for information purposes, subject to such limitation as security and constitutional considerations may require, statistical and other information of a technical nature relating to economic, social, and educational conditions in the territories for which they are respectively responsible other than those territories to which Chapters XII and XIII apply.

Article 74.

Members of the United Nations also agree that their policy in respect of the territories to which this Chapter applies, no less than in respect of their metropolitan areas, must be based on the general principle of good-neighbourliness, due account being taken of the interests and well-being of the rest of the world, in social, economic, and commercial matters.

Chapter XII
International Trusteeship System

Article 75.

The United Nations shall establish under its authority an international trusteeship system for the administration and supervision of such territories as may be placed thereunder by subsequent individual agreements. These territories are hereinafter referred to as trust territories.

Article 76.

The basic objectives of the trusteeship system, in accordance with the Purposes of the United Nations laid down in Article 1 of the present Charter, shall be:

A. to further international peace and security;
B. to promote the political, economic, social, and educational advancement of the inhabitants of the trust territories, and their progressive development towards self-government or independence as may be appropriate to the particular circumstances of each territory and its peoples and the freely expressed wishes of the peoples concerned, and as may be provided by the terms of each trusteeship agreement;
C. to encourage respect for human rights and for fundamental freedoms for all without distinction as to race, sex, language, or religion, and to encourage recognition of the interdependence of the peoples of the world; and
D. to ensure equal treatment in social, economic, and commercial matters for all Members of the United Nations and their nationals, and also equal treatment for the latter in the administration of justice, without prejudice to the attainment of the foregoing objectives and subject to the provisions of Article 80.

Article 77.

1. The trusteeship system shall apply to such territories in the following categories as may be placed thereunder by means of trusteeship agreements:
    A. territories now held under mandate;
    B. territories which may be detached from enemy states as a result of the Second World War; and
    C. territories voluntarily placed under the system by states responsible for their administration.
2. It will be a matter for subsequent agreement as to which territories in the foregoing categories will be brought under the trusteeship system and upon what terms.

Article 78.

The trusteeship system shall not apply to territories which have become Members of the United Nations, relationship among which shall be based on respect for the principle of sovereign equality.

Article 79.

The terms of trusteeship for each territory to be placed under the trusteeship system, including any alteration or amendment, shall be agreed upon by the states directly concerned, including the mandatory power in the case of territories held under mandate by a Member of the United Nations, and shall be approved as provided for in Articles 83 and 85.

Article 80.

1. Except as may be agreed upon in individual trusteeship agreements, made under Articles 77, 79, and 81, placing each territory under the

trusteeship system, and until such agreements have been concluded, nothing in this Chapter shall be construed in or of itself to alter in any manner the rights whatsoever of any states or any peoples or the terms of existing international instruments to which Members of the United Nations may respectively be parties.

2. Paragraph 1 of this Article shall not be interpreted as giving grounds for delay or postponement of the negotiation and conclusion of agreements for placing mandated and other territories under the trusteeship system as provided for in Article 77.

Article 81.

The trusteeship agreement shall in each case include the terms under which the trust territory will be administered and designate the authority which will exercise the administration of the trust territory. Such authority, hereinafter called the administering authority, may be one or more states or the Organization itself.

Article 82.

There may be designated, in any trusteeship agreement, a strategic area or areas which may include part or all of the trust territory to which the agreement applies, without prejudice to any special agreement or agreements made under Article 43.

Article 83.

1. All functions of the United Nations relating to strategic areas, including the approval of the terms of the trusteeship agreements and of their alteration or amendment shall be exercised by the Security Council.
2. The basic objectives set forth in Article 76 shall be applicable to the people of each strategic area.
3. The Security Council shall, subject to the provisions of the trusteeship agreements and without prejudice to security considerations, avail itself of the assistance of the Trusteeship Council to perform those functions of the United Nations under the trusteeship system relating to political, economic, social, and educational matters in the strategic areas.

Article 84.

It shall be the duty of the administering authority to ensure that the trust territory shall play its part in the maintenance of international peace and security. To this end the administering authority may make use of volunteer forces, facilities, and assistance from the trust territory in carrying out the obligations towards the Security Council undertaken in this regard by the administering authority, as well as for local defence and the maintenance of law and order within the trust territory.

Article 85.

1. The functions of the United Nations with regard to trusteeship agreements for all areas not designated as strategic, including the

approval of the terms of the trusteeship agreements and of their alteration or amendment, shall be exercised by the General Assembly.

2. The Trusteeship Council, operating under the authority of the General Assembly shall assist the General Assembly in carrying out these functions.

Chapter XIII
The Trusteeship Council

Composition

Article 86.

1. The Trusteeship Council shall consist of the following Members of the United Nations:

    A. those Members administering trust territories;
    B. such of those Members mentioned by name in Article 23 as are not administering trust territories; and
    C. as many other Members elected for three-year terms by the General Assembly as may be necessary to ensure that the total number of members of the Trusteeship Council is equally divided between those Members of the United Nations which administer trust territories and those which do not.

2. Each member of the Trusteeship Council shall designate one specially qualified person to represent it therein.

Functions and Powers

Article 87.

The General Assembly and, under its authority, the Trusteeship Council, in carrying out their functions, may:

A. consider reports submitted by the administering authority;
B. accept petitions and examine them in consultation with the administering authority;
C. provide for periodic visits to the respective trust territories at times agreed upon with the administering authority; and
D. take these and other actions in conformity with the terms of the trusteeship agreements.

Article 88.

The Trusteeship Council shall formulate a questionnaire on the political, economic, social, and educational advancement of the inhabitants of each trust territory, and the administering authority for each trust territory within the competence of the General Assembly shall make an annual report to the General Assembly upon the basis of such questionnaire.

Voting

Article 89.

1. Each member of the Trusteeship Council shall have one vote.
2. Decisions of the Trusteeship Council shall be made by a majority of the members present and voting.

Procedure

Article 90.

1. The Trusteeship Council shall adopt its own rules of procedure, including the method of selecting its President.
2. The Trusteeship Council shall meet as required in accordance with its rules, which shall include provision for the convening of meetings on the request of a majority of its members.

Article 91.

The Trusteeship Council shall, when appropriate, avail itself of the assistance of the Economic and Social Council and of the specialized agencies in regard to matters with which they are respectively concerned.

Chapter XIV
The International Court of Justice

Article 92.

The International Court of Justice shall be the principal judicial organ of the United Nations. It shall function in accordance with the annexed Statute, which is based upon the Statute of the Permanent Court of International Justice and forms an integral part of the present Charter.

Article 93.

1. All Members of the United Nations are ipso facto parties to the Statute of the International Court of Justice.
2. A state which is not a Member of the United Nations may become a party to the Statute of the International Court of Justice on conditions to be determined in each case by the General Assembly upon the recommendation of the Security Council.

Article 94.

1. Each Member of the United Nations undertakes to comply with the decision of the International Court of Justice in any case to which it is a party.

2. If any party to a case fails to perform the obligations incumbent upon it under a judgment rendered by the Court, the other party may have recourse to the Security Council, which may, if it deems necessary, make recommendations or decide upon measures to be taken to give effect to the judgment.

Article 95.

Nothing in the present Charter shall prevent Members of the United Nations from entrusting the solution of their differences to other tribunals by virtue of agreements already in existence or which may be concluded in the future.

Article 96.

1. The General Assembly or the Security Council may request the International Court of Justice to give an advisory opinion on any legal question.
2. Other organs of the United Nations and specialized agencies, which may at any time be so authorized by the General Assembly, may also request advisory opinions of the Court on legal questions arising within the scope of their activities.

Chapter XV
The Secretariat

Article 97.

The Secretariat shall comprise a Secretary-General and such staff as the Organization may require. The Secretary-General shall be appointed by the General Assembly upon the recommendation of the Security Council. He shall be the chief administrative officer of the Organization.

Article 98.

The Secretary-General shall act in that capacity in all meetings of the General Assembly, of the Security Council, of the Economic and Social Council, and of the Trusteeship Council, and shall perform such other functions as are entrusted to him by these organs. The Secretary-General shall make an annual report to the General Assembly on the work of the Organization.

Article 99.

The Secretary-General may bring to the attention of the Security Council any matter which in his opinion may threaten the maintenance of international peace and security.

Article 100.

1. In the performance of their duties the Secretary-General and the staff shall not seek or receive instructions from any government or from any other authority external to the Organization. They shall refrain from any

action which might reflect on their position as international officials responsible only to the Organization.

2. Each Member of the United Nations undertakes to respect the exclusively international character of the responsibilities of the Secretary-General and the staff and not to seek to influence them in the discharge of their responsibilities.

Article 101.

1. The staff shall be appointed by the Secretary-General under regulations established by the General Assembly.
2. Appropriate staffs shall be permanently assigned to the Economic and Social Council, the Trusteeship Council, and, as required, to other organs of the United Nations. These staffs shall form a part of the Secretariat.
3. The paramount consideration in the employment of the staff and in the determination of the conditions of service shall be the necessity of securing the highest standards of efficiency, competence, and integrity. Due regard shall be paid to the importance of recruiting the staff on as wide a geographical basis as possible.

Chapter XVI
Miscellaneous Provisions

Article 102.

1. Every treaty and every international agreement entered into by any Member of the United Nations after the present Charter comes into force shall as soon as possible be registered with the Secretariat and published by it.
2. No party to any such treaty or international agreement which has not been registered in accordance with the provisions of paragraph 1 of this Article may invoke that treaty or agreement before any organ of the United Nations.

Article 103.

In the event of a conflict between the obligations of the Members of the United Nations under the present Charter and their obligations under any other international agreement, their obligations under the present Charter shall prevail.

Article 104.

The Organization shall enjoy in the territory of each of its Members such legal capacity as may be necessary for the exercise of its functions and the fulfilment of its purposes.

Article 105.

1. The Organization shall enjoy in the territory of each of its Members such privileges and immunities as are necessary for the fulfilment of its purposes.

2. Representatives of the Members of the United Nations and officials of the Organization shall similarly enjoy such privileges and immunities as are necessary for the independent exercise of their functions in connexion with the Organization.

3. The General Assembly may make recommendations with a view to determining the details of the application of paragraphs 1 and 2 of this Article or may propose conventions to the Members of the United Nations for this purpose.

Chapter XVII
Transitional Security Arrangements

Article 106.

Pending the coming into force of such special agreements referred to in Article 43 as in the opinion of the Security Council enable it to begin the exercise of its responsibilities under Article 42, the parties to the Four-Nation Declaration, signed at Moscow, 30 October 1943, and France, shall, in accordance with the provisions of paragraph 5 of that Declaration, consult with one another and as occasion requires with other Members of the United Nations with a view to such joint action on behalf of the Organization as may be necessary for the purpose of maintaining international peace and security.

Article 107.

Nothing in the present Charter shall invalidate or preclude action, in relation to any state which during the Second World War has been an enemy of any signatory to the present Charter, taken or authorized as a result of that war by the Governments having responsibility for such action.

Chapter XVIII
Amendments

Article 108.

Amendments to the present Charter shall come into force for all Members of the United Nations when they have been adopted by a vote of two thirds of the members of the General Assembly and ratified in accordance with their respective constitutional processes by two thirds of the Members of the United Nations, including all the permanent members of the Security Council.

Article 109.

1. A General Conference of the Members of the United Nations for the purpose of reviewing the present Charter may be held at a date and place to be fixed by a two-thirds vote of the members of the General Assembly and by a vote of any nine members of the Security Council.

      Each Member of the United Nations shall have one vote in the conference.

2. Any alteration of the present Charter recommended by a two-thirds vote of the conference shall take effect when ratified in accordance with their respective constitutional processes by two thirds of the Members of the United Nations including all the permanent members of the Security Council.

3. If such a conference has not been held before the tenth annual session of the General Assembly following the coming into force of the present Charter, the proposal to call such a conference shall be placed on the agenda of that session of the General Assembly, and the conference shall be held if so decided by a majority vote of the members of the General Assembly and by a vote of any seven members of the Security Council.

Chapter XIX
Ratification and Signature

Article 110.

1. The present Charter shall be ratified by the signatory states in accordance with their respective constitutional processes.

2. The ratifications shall be deposited with the Government of the United States of America, which shall notify all the signatory states of each deposit as well as the Secretary-General of the Organization when he has been appointed.

3. The present Charter shall come into force upon the deposit of ratifications by the Republic of China, France, the Union of Soviet Socialist Republics, the United Kingdom of Great Britain and Northern Ireland, and the United States of America, and by a majority of the other signatory states. A protocol of the ratifications deposited shall thereupon be drawn up by the Government of the United States of America which shall communicate copies thereof to all the signatory states.

4. The states signatory to the present Charter which ratify it after it has come into force will become original Members of the United Nations on the date of the deposit of their respective ratifications.

Article 111.

The present Charter, of which the Chinese, French, Russian, English, and Spanish texts are equally authentic, shall remain deposited in the archives of the Government of the United States of America. Duly certified copies thereof shall be transmitted by that Government to the Governments of the other signatory states.

IN FAITH WHEREOF the representatives of the Governments of the United Nations have signed the present Charter.

DONE at the city of San Francisco the twenty-sixth day of June, one thousand nine hundred and forty-five.

Notes

Chapter 1

1. On the historical background of collective security, particularly the absence of similarly based, operative systems before the League of Nations, see Joel Larus, *From Collective Security to Preventive Diplomacy* (New York: John Wiley, 1965), pp. 1–5; Inis L. Claude Jr., *Swords into Plowshares: The Problems and Progress of International Organization,* 3rd ed. (New York: Random House, 1964), p. 20; and Inis L. Claude Jr., *Power and International Relations* (New York: Random House, 1962), pp. 106–108.

2. Quoted in Larus, *From Collective Security,* p. 2.

3. Ibid., p. 3.

4. Ibid., p. 4.

5. For a lucid analysis of the Westphalian system and its implications for balance-of-power politics, see Lynn H. Miller, *Global Order: Values and Power in International Politics* (Boulder: Westview Press, 1990), chap. 2.

6. See Henry Kissinger, *Diplomacy* (New York: Simon and Schuster, 1994), pp. 77–79.

7. Quoted in Hamilton Foley, *Woodrow Wilson's Case for the League of Nations* (Princeton: Princeton University Press, 1923), p. 8.

8. A. J. P. Taylor, *English History, 1914–1945* (New York: Oxford University Press, 1965), p. 133.

9. On the French position, see Stephen S. Goodspeed, *The Nature and Function of International Organization,* 2nd ed. (New York: Oxford University Press, 1967), p. 32; and Ernst B. Haas and Allen S. Whiting, *Dynamics of International Relations* (New York: McGraw-Hill, 1956), p. 464.

10. Foley, *Woodrow Wilson's Case,* p. 10.

11. Stanley Hoffmann, "The Future of the International Political System: A Sketch," in *Global Dilemmas,* edited by Samuel P. Huntington and Joseph S. Nye (Cambridge, Mass.: Center for International Affairs, 1985), p. 281.

12. Robert E. Riggs and Jack C. Plano, *The United Nations: International Organization and World Politics* (Chicago: The Dorsey Press, 1988), p. 4.

Chapter 2

1. The automaticity of economic sanctions in the event of noncompliance with the League's peaceful-settlement provisions was diluted in 1921 by an agreed interpretation of the covenant under which each member had the right to decide

for itself whether to apply economic and other sanctions in the event of aggression. See Robert E. Riggs and Jack C. Plano, *The United Nations: International Organization and World Politics* (Chicago: The Dorsey Press, 1988), p. 10.

2. Gary B. Ostrower, *Collective Insecurity: The United States and the League of Nations During the Early Thirties* (Lewisburg, Pa.: Bucknell University Press, 1979), p. 37.

3. See Ruth B. Russell, *A History of the United Nations Charter: The Role of the United States 1940–1945* (Washington, D.C.: The Brookings Institution, 1958), p. 646; and Leland M. Goodrich and Edvard Hambro, *Charter of the United Nations: Commentary and Documents* (Boston: World Peace Foundation, 1946), p. 122.

4. See Evan Luard, *A History of the United Nations: The Years of Western Domination, 1945–1955* (New York: St. Martin's Press, 1982), chap. 1, for an analysis of the lessons of the League as perceived by the framers of the UN Charter.

5. For discussions of the League's peaceful-settlement activities, see James Avery Joyce, *Broken Star: The Story of the League of Nations, 1919–1939* (Swansea: Christopher Davies, 1975), chaps. 4, 5; *Encyclopaedia Britannica*, 13th ed., s.v. "League of Nations"; and Ernst B. Haas and Allen S. Whiting, *Dynamics of International Relations* (New York: McGraw-Hill, 1956), p. 465.

6. *The New Encyclopedia Britannica*, 15th ed., s.v. "International Relations."

7. For an account of the procedures followed by the League of Nations Council and Assembly in the Ethiopian problem, see Stephen S. Goodspeed, *The Nature and Function of International Organization*, 2nd ed. (New York: Oxford University Press, 1967), p. 56.

8. Harold Nicolson, *Diaries and Letters*, vol. 1, *1930–1939*, edited by Nigel Nicolson (New York: Atheneum, 1966), p. 230.

9. On the domestic politics and purposes of the Neutrality Acts, see Charles Warren, "Congress and Neutrality," in *Neutrality and Collective Security*, edited by Quincy Wright (Chicago: The University of Chicago Press, 1936), pp. 109–153.

10. Riggs and Plano, *United Nations*, p. 20.

11. On the consequences of the Western democracies' abandonment of collective security, and of U.S. neutrality in particular, see Sir Alfred Zimmern, "The Problem of Collective Security," in *Neutrality and Collective Security*, edited by Quincy Wright (Chicago: The University of Chicago Press, 1936), p. 5 and passim.

12. Quoted in Nicolson, *Diaries and Letters*, vol. 1, p. 393.

Chapter 3

1. Harold Nicolson, *Diaries and Letters*, vol. 2, *The War Years, 1939–1945*, edited by Nigel Nicolson (New York: Atheneum, 1967), p. 449.

2. Evan Luard, *A History of the United Nations: The Years of Western Domination, 1945–1955* (New York: St. Martin's Press, 1982), p. 21.

3. Quoted in Inis L. Claude Jr., *Swords into Plowshares: The Problems and Progress of International Organization*, 4th ed. (New York: Random House, 1971), p. 113. The passage is from a speech of May 7, 1948, in which Churchill spoke about his wartime views.

4. See Gordon A. Craig and Alexander L. George, *Force and Statecraft: Diplomatic Problems of Our Time* (New York: Oxford University Press, 1983), pp.

108–110. The authors argue that Roosevelt regarded a return to the post-Napoleonic concert system as the realistic middle ground between a balance-of-power system, which he regarded as no longer workable, and an overly idealistic collective-security system based on the League of Nations. For an account of Woodrow Wilson's similar views on the need for a "concert of power" or "community of power" to make collective security workable, see Inis L. Claude Jr., *Power and International Relations* (New York: Random House, 1962), pp. 96–97.

5. Arthur H. Vandenberg Jr., ed., *The Private Papers of Senator Vandenberg* (Boston: Houghton Mifflin, 1952), p. 1. Vandenberg was one of the few participants in the charter negotiations to stress the connection between collective security and the protection of U.S. national interests in Asia. In the early 1940s the point may have been too obvious to need articulation.

6. Ruth B. Russell, *A History of the United Nations Charter: The Role of the United States 1940–1945* (Washington, D.C.: The Brookings Institution, 1958), p. 686.

7. See A. J. P. Taylor, *English History, 1914–1945* (New York: Oxford University Press, 1965), p. 601.

8. Pertinent portions of this letter are quoted in Russell, *History of the United Nations Charter,* p. 181.

9. Ibid., p. 686.

10. Although the first atomic weapon that the Soviets exploded, in August 1949, was built from plans of the earliest U.S. bomb provided by Klaus Fuchs, the USSR detonated a lighter and more powerful version of its own in 1951. Soviet scientists who helped develop the 1949 and 1951 bombs have said since the end of the Cold War that the USSR used all of the plutonium it possessed in the 1949 weapon. Hence, except for a brief period in early 1949, the U.S. nuclear-weapons monopoly lasted until 1951. See *New York Times,* January 14, 1993, p. 12.

11. Russell, *History of the United Nations Charter,* pp. 94, 125, 194.

12. Ibid., p. 126.

13. Ibid., p. 200.

14. Vandenberg, *Private Papers,* p. 111.

15. Quoted in Claude, *Swords into Plowshares,* p. 74.

16. See Robert C. Hilderbrand, *Dumbarton Oaks: The Origins of the United Nations and the Search for Postwar Security* (Chapel Hill: The University of North Carolina Press, 1990), pp. 25, 32; and Russell, *History of the United Nations Charter,* pp. 98, 227, 247–249, 293–294.

17. Hilderbrand, *Dumbarton Oaks,* pp. 35, 36.

18. Claude, *Swords into Plowshares,* p. 143.

19. Hilderbrand, *Dumbarton Oaks,* p. 57.

20. Vandenberg, *Private Papers,* pp. 95–96. The italics are Vandenberg's.

21. Claude, *Swords into Plowshares,* p. 72.

22. Hilderbrand, *Dumbarton Oaks,* p. 149.

23. Ibid.

24. See Bruce Russett and James S. Sutterlin, "The U.N. in a New World Order," *Foreign Affairs* (Spring 1991), p. 78.

25. Hilderbrand, *Dumbarton Oaks,* p. 152.

26. Leland M. Goodrich and Edvard Hambro, *Charter of the United Nations: Commentary and Documents* (Boston: World Peace Foundation, 1946), p. 168.

27. See Hilderbrand, *Dumbarton Oaks*, pp. 21–23, 140–143.

28. U.S. Department of State, *Foreign Relations of the United States, 1946*, vol. 1, *General: The United Nations* (Washington, D.C.: U.S. Government Printing Office, 1972), p. 719.

29. Goodrich and Hambro, *Charter of the United Nations*, p. 129.

30. Trygve Lie, *In the Cause of Peace* (New York: Macmillan, 1954), p. 98.

31. Claude, *Swords into Plowshares*, p. 78.

32. UN General Assembly Resolution 1991 A (XVIII), December 17, 1963; 18 GAOR, Supp. 15, pp. 21–22. The affirmative votes of the permanent members are required for charter amendment; thus, although the General Assembly passed a resolution to enlarge the Security Council in December 1963, the amendment did not come into force until August 31, 1965, when the United States deposited its instrument of ratification. See *UN Monthly Chronicle*, vol. 2 (August-September 1965), pp. 24–25.

Chapter 4

1. Clement R. Attlee, *Collective Security Under the United Nations* (London: The David Davies Memorial Institute of International Studies, 1958), p. 3.

2. See Kenneth W. Thompson, *Political Realism and the Crisis of World Politics: An American Approach to Foreign Policy* (Princeton: Princeton University Press, 1960), p. 19.

3. Hans J. Morgenthau, ed., *Peace, Security, and the United Nations* (Chicago: The University of Chicago Press, 1946), p. 7 of preface.

4. Hans J. Morgenthau, *Politics Among Nations: The Struggle for Power and Peace*, 5th ed. (New York: Knopf, 1973), p. 5.

5. Ibid.

6. Thompson, *Political Realism*, p. 36.

7. Nicholas J. Spykman, *The Geography of the Peace* (New York: Harcourt, Brace, 1944), p. 4.

8. Ibid.

9. On the changing nature of interdependence since World War II, see Robert O. Keohane and Joseph S. Nye, *Power and Interdependence: World Politics in Transition* (Boston: Little, Brown, 1977), p. 3 and passim; and Robert O. Keohane and Joseph S. Nye, "Power and Interdependence Revisited," *International Organization* (Autumn 1987).

10. See, for example, Hans J. Morgenthau and Kenneth W. Thompson, eds., *Principles and Problems of International Politics* (New York: Knopf, 1952), p. 222; Morgenthau, *Politics Among Nations*, pp. 65, 132; Thompson, *Political Realism*, p. 7; and Morgenthau, *A New Foreign Policy* (New York: Praeger, 1969), pp. 129–130.

11. George F. Kennan, "The Sources of Soviet Conduct," *Foreign Affairs* (Spring 1987), p. 816. Reprinted from *Foreign Affairs* (July 1947), in which the article was published under the pseudonym "X."

12. George F. Kennan, *Russia, the Atom and the West* (New York: Harper, 1957), p. 17.

13. Remarking on the "severe limitations . . . [of the] 'realist' picture of the world," Samuel Huntington observes that "the interests of states are also shaped

... by their domestic values and institutions. . . ." In an insight that weakens his thesis that the clash of great civilizations is virtually predestined, he continues that "values, culture, and institutions, . . . [including] international norms and institutions . . . , pervasively influence how states define their interests." One may hope that avoiding a nuclear holocaust will continue to be the most pervasive of all national interests, in the future as it has been in the recent past. Samuel Huntington, *The Clash of Civilizations and the Remaking of the World Order* (New York: Simon & Schuster, 1996), p. 34.

14. See, for example, George F. Kennan, *Memoirs, 1925–1950* (Boston: Little, Brown, 1967), p. 559; Kennan, "Sources of Soviet Conduct," p. 867; George F. Kennan, "Foreign Aid in the Framework of National Policy," in *Principles and Problems of International Politics,* edited by Hans J. Morgenthau and Kenneth W. Thompson (New York: Knopf, 1952), pp. 222, 226; George F. Kennan, "Is War with Russia Inevitable?" in *Principles and Problems of International Politics,* edited by Hans J. Morgenthau and Kenneth W. Thompson (New York: Knopf, 1952), p. 379; Kennan, *Russia, the Atom and the West,* pp. 13–14; and George F. Kennan, *Around the Cragged Hill* (New York: W. W. Norton, 1993), pp. 180–184.

15. Kennan, *Russia, the Atom and the West,* p. 13.

16. See Thompson, *Political Realism,* pp. 50–61, for an analysis of the efforts of Kennan and other State Department policy planning officials to develop a realistic theoretical framework for U.S. foreign policy during the Cold War.

17. On the various usages of the term "balance of power," see Inis L. Claude Jr., *Power and International Relations* (New York: Random House, 1962), chaps. 2, 3; and Robert E. Riggs and Jack C. Plano, *The United Nations: International Organization and World Politics* (Chicago: The Dorsey Press, 1988), chap. 5.

18. Morgenthau, *Politics Among Nations,* p. 174.

19. Henry A. Kissinger, "False Dreams of a New World Order," *Washington Post,* February 26, 1991.

20. Raymond Aron, *Le Grand Débat. Initiation à la stratégie atomique* (Paris: Calmann-Lévy, 1962), p. 209 (my translation). On the same point, see Raymond Aron, *The Dawn of Universal History* (New York: Praeger, 1961), p. 54.

21. Aron, *Le Grand Débat,* p. 210.

22. Quoted in Inis L. Claude Jr., *Swords into Plowshares: The Problems and Progress of International Organization,* 4th ed. (New York: Random House, 1971), p. 291.

23. Henry A. Kissinger, "Domestic Structure and Foreign Policy," in *Conditions of World Order,* edited by Stanley Hoffmann (Boston: Houghton Mifflin, 1968), p. 187. The special problems that flow from the spread of nuclear weapons to the middle powers are discussed in Harlan Cleveland, "The Evolution of Rising Responsibility," in *The United Nations in the Balance,* edited by Norman J. Padelford and Leland M. Goodrich (New York: Praeger, 1965).

24. On the changes in international politics caused by the fear of escalation to nuclear war, see Stanley Hoffmann, *Primacy or World Order: American Foreign Policy Since the Cold War* (New York: McGraw-Hill, 1978), pp. 172–173.

25. Stanley Hoffmann, "Obstinate or Obsolete? The Fate of the Nation-State and the Case of Modern Europe," in *Conditions of World Order,* edited by Stanley Hoffmann (Boston: Houghton Mifflin, 1968), p. 113.

26. Claude, *Power and International Relations*, p. 194.

27. Quoted in Anwar Hussain Syed, *Walter Lippmann's Philosophy of International Politics* (Philadelphia: The University of Pennsylvania Press, 1963), p. 108.

28. See Riggs and Plano, *United Nations*, p. 125; and Claude, *Swords into Plowshares*, pp. 256–259.

29. See Inis L. Claude Jr., "Implications and Questions for the Future," in *The United Nations in the Balance*, edited by Norman J. Padelford and Leland M. Goodrich (New York: Praeger, 1965), p. 473.

30. On China's exclusion from the UN during the Korean War, Aron remarks that "there was every reason to exclude China if one looks to the principles of the UN Charter but every reason to admit it if one wishes the UN to be a place of dialogue." Raymond Aron, *La Guerre froide. Les articles de politique internationale dans Le Figaro de 1947 à 1977* (Paris: Éditions de Fallois, 1990), p. 763 (my translation).

31. For different opinions about the kinds of "consensus" needed for effective collective security, see Leland M. Goodrich, *The United Nations* (New York: Crowell, 1959), p. 164; Thompson, *Political Realism*, p. 192; Jack C. Plano and Robert E. Riggs, *Forging World Order: The Politics of International Organization* (New York: Macmillan, 1967), p. 249; and Claude, *Swords into Plowshares*, pp. 250–253.

32. Unlike most trends in international politics, the developing world's shift toward pragmatism has a conspicuous watershed: the General Assembly's repeal in 1991 of the Arab/Nonaligned/Soviet bloc–supported General Assembly resolution of November 1975 equating Zionism with racism. For a discussion of the ideological politics that generated the resolution, see Daniel Patrick Moynihan, *A Dangerous Place* (Boston: Little, Brown, 1975), chaps. 9, 11. For Hans Morgenthau's view of the resolution, see John G. Stoessinger, "The Statesman and the Critic: Kissinger and Morgenthau," in *A Tribute to Hans Morgenthau*, edited by Kenneth W. Thompson and Robert Myers (Washington, D.C.: The New Republic Book Company, 1977), p. 230.

33. Henry A. Kissinger, *Nuclear Weapons and Foreign Policy* (New York: Harper, 1957), p. 246. See also Henry A. Kissinger, *The Necessity for Choice* (Garden City, N.Y.: Doubleday, 1962), p. 120, for a discussion of Western alliance problems caused by "the very essence of sovereignty [being] the right to take independent action."

34. Kissinger, *Nuclear Weapons*, p. 247.

35. Walter Lippmann, *New York Herald Tribune*, January 15, 1951.

36. Aron, *Le Grand Débat*, p. 206.

37. Ibid., p. 207.

38. Quoted in Raymond Aron, *Main Currents in Sociological Thought* (London: Pelican Books, 1968), p. 230.

39. Walter Lippmann, *Essays in the Public Philosophy* (Boston: Little, Brown, 1955), p. 19. For an examination of Lippmann's views on the uses of collective force, see Raymond Aron, *The Imperial Republic: The United States and the World 1945–1973* (New York: University Press of America, 1974), p. 298.

40. Raymond Aron, "Limits to the Powers of the United Nations," *Annals of the American Academy of Political and Social Sciences* (November 1954), p. 26.

41. Ibid., p. 20.

42. Ibid.

43. The chief point of contention was whether the term "aggression," as used in Chapter VII of the UN Charter, encompasses the use of armed force by national liberation groups against colonial regimes. The final, agreed definition answered in the negative. Article 7 of the definition excludes from "aggression" acts by and in support of peoples struggling to achieve "self-determination, freedom and independence" from "colonial and racist regimes or other forms of alien domination."

44. Raymond Aron, *Paix et Guerre entre les nations* (Paris: Calmann-Lévy, 1962), pp. 571–572 (my translation; Aron's italics).

Chapter 5

1. The MSC talks were limited to the military implications of Article 43 and were negotiated by senior officers of the armed forces of the permanent-member states. General Matthew B. Ridgway represented the United States. In a number of respects, the military positions were more apolitical and accommodating than those of the State Department. In 1946, for example, there was a running debate in the U.S. government on how hard to press the Soviets for a position on the makeup of an international force. The U.S. delegation argued that high-level pressure would damage its relations with the Soviet delegation and obstruct agreement, and, for the better part of a year, that point of view prevailed. See U.S. Department of State, *Foreign Relations of the United States, 1946,* vol. 1, *General: The United Nations* (Washington, D.C.: U.S. Government Printing Office, 1972), pp. 784, 790, 875.

2. Department of State, *Foreign Relations,* vol. 1, p. 759.

3. United Nations Department of Public Information, Press Division, *Press Release* MSC/28, September 9, 1947.

4. For a more detailed account of the permanent members' positions on the character of a UN military force, see Leland M. Goodrich and Anne P. Simons, *The United Nations and the Maintenance of International Peace and Security* (Washington, D.C.: The Brookings Institution, 1955), pp. 398–405.

5. Inis L. Claude Jr., "The United Nations and the Use of Force," *International Conciliation* (March 1961), p. 349.

6. Raymond Aron regards the "paralysis of the . . . meetings" not as a consequence of the Cold War but as one of the first events that precipitated it, along with what "Washington saw as . . . the USSR's abuse of influence in Eastern Europe and the sovietization of its occupation zone in Germany." Raymond Aron, *Le Grand Schisme* (Paris: Gallimard, 1948), p. 33 (my translation).

7. See Robert Jervis, "From Balance to Concert: A Study of International Security Cooperation," *World Politics* (October 1985), p. 58. Jervis considers 1945–1946 to be one of the three concert-of-power periods in modern history, the other two being from 1815 to 1822 and from 1919 to 1920.

8. Department of State, *Foreign Relations,* vol. 1, p. 718.

9. Ibid., p. 769.

10. Ibid., pp. 769, 779, passim.

11. Ibid., p. 779.

12. Ibid.

13. Quoted in Donald C. Blaisdell, *Arms for the United Nations* (Washington, D.C.: U.S. Department of State, 1948), p. 17.

14. Department of State, *Foreign Relations*, vol. 1, p. 779.

15. See Evan Luard, *Conflict and Peace in the Modern International System* (Boston: Little, Brown, 1968), p. 237.

16. Department of State, *Foreign Relations*, vol. 1, p. 773.

17. This and other controversies that arose in the MSC talks are discussed in Claude, "United Nations," p. 352, passim.

18. These points are a paraphrase and summary of the MSC report of April 30, 1947, entitled "Report on General Principles Governing the Organization of the Armed Forces to Be Made Available to the Security Council by Member Nations of the United Nations" (S/336). The report is attached to S/366, dated June 4, 1947, which is in turn published in *Yearbook of the United Nations 1946–1947* (Lake Success, N.Y.: United Nations Department of Public Information, 1947), pp. 422ff.

19. Department of State, *Foreign Relations*, vol. 1, pp. 759–760.

20. A case in point is Soviet advocacy of a standing, integrated UN air corps during early great-power discussions, because of the quick reaction time and the punishment it could inflict on the populations of aggressor states. See Robert C. Hilderbrand, *Dumbarton Oaks: The Origins of the United Nations and the Search for Postwar Security* (Chapel Hill: The University of North Carolina Press, 1990), p. 142. By June 1947, when the Security Council discussed the MSC "Report on General Principles," the USSR was no longer prepared to support a special degree of readiness for national air force units. See Andrei Gromyko's statement to the Security Council on June 6, 1947 (Security Council Official Records, Second Year No. 44, 139th Meeting, June 6, 1947).

21. Department of State, *Foreign Relations*, vol. 1, p. 776.

22. Ibid.

Chapter 6

1. Interestingly, but almost certainly coincidentally, the Soviet boycott began the day after Secretary of State Dean Acheson, in a speech before the National Press Club on January 12, 1950, defined the U.S. "defense perimeter" in the Pacific without including Korea. Acheson notes in his memoirs that General Douglas MacArthur used similar language to describe U.S. defensive dispositions in Asia the previous year, on March 1, 1949. See Dean Acheson, *Present at the Creation: My Years in the State Department* (New York: W. W. Norton, 1969), p. 357.

2. Henry Kissinger, *Diplomacy* (New York: Simon and Schuster, 1994), p. 477.

3. In 1975, during a closed session of the Security Council, Ambassador Malik, who was again serving as Soviet ambassador to the UN, asked me to my surprise to move up to the U.S. representative's seat (the senior delegate having been called away for a moment). To the amusement of the other members, Malik remarked that ever since 1950 he had been uncomfortable when a permanent member did not participate fully in the council's proceedings.

4. Raymond Aron, *Paix et Guerre entre les nations* (Paris: Calmann-Lévy, 1962), p. 546 (my translation).

5. The Soviets maintained that the July 7 resolution was also invalid because it was "passed by participation of the Chinese Nationalists." See Clyde Eagleton and Richard N. Swift, eds., *Annual Review of United Nations Affairs, 1950* (New York: New York University Press, 1951), p. 138.

6. On the implications of abstention and absence in Security Council voting, see Tae-Ho Yoo, *The Korean War and the United Nations: A Legal and Diplomatic Study* (Louvain, France: Université Catholique de Louvain, 1964), pp. 109–110.

7. See Stephen S. Goodspeed, *The Nature and Function of International Organization,* 2nd ed. (New York: Oxford University Press, 1967), p. 253.

8. Raymond Aron, *La Guerre froide. Les articles de politique internationale dans Le Figaro de 1947 à 1977* (Paris: Éditions de Fallois, 1990), pp. 587–588 (my translation).

9. General Assembly Resolution 377(V), November 3, 1950.

10. For an overview of the peace initiatives from various groups in the General Assembly, see Dean Acheson, "Oral Report Delivered Before the Political and Security Committee of the United Nations General Assembly on October 24, 1952," Department of State Publication 4771 (Washington, D.C.: U.S. Government Printing Office, 1952), pp. 22–24. On India's leading role in the search for a compromise settlement, see Marc Frankenstein, "Les initiatives de l'Inde pour le règlement du conflit coréen," *Revue Politique et Parlementaire* (July 1951).

11. Goodspeed, *International Organization,* p. 259. For a more detailed discussion of the General Assembly's reluctance to declare China an aggressor or impose serious sanctions on it, see Leland M. Goodrich, *The United Nations in a Changing World* (New York: Columbia University Press, 1974), p. 73ff.

12. Acheson, *Present at the Creation,* p. 447.

13. Leland M. Goodrich, "Korea: Collective Measures Against Aggression," *International Conciliation* (October 1953), p. 165.

14. Ibid., p. 167.

15. Leland M. Goodrich, *Korea: A Study of U.S. Policy in the United Nations* (New York: Council on Foreign Relations, 1956), p. 118.

16. See Acheson, *Present at the Creation,* pp. 450, 531. The quotation is from a speech by Acheson to the Newspaper Guild on June 29, 1950.

17. Ibid., p. 445.

18. At Senate hearings in May 1951 after General MacArthur's relief, General Omar N. Bradley was asked whether the second UN offensive would stop at the line where North Korean aggression began. He replied: "We are fighting an action without regard to the thirty-eighth parallel if necessary." Senate Committees on Armed Services and Foreign Relations, *Hearings to Conduct an Inquiry into the Military Situation in the Far East and the Facts Surrounding the Relief of General of the Army Douglas MacArthur from His Assignments in That Area,* 82nd Congress, 1st session (Washington, D.C.: U.S. Government Printing Office, 1951), pt. 2, p. 938 (hereafter cited as *MacArthur Hearings*).

19. The cease-fire proposal was transmitted to Soviet UN Ambassador Jacob Malik by George Kennan, who "spoke only vaguely of a cease-fire line" at a time when the UN forces under General Ridgway were deployed both to the north

and south of the parallel. In retrospect it seemed to Acheson that "the Russians and Chinese could well have been surprised, chagrined, and given cause to feel tricked when . . . we revealed a firm determination as a matter of major principle not to accept the 38th parallel as the armistice line." Acheson, *Present at the Creation*, pp. 532, 536.

20. *MacArthur Hearings*, pt. 1, p. 30.

21. For a thoughtful portrayal of MacArthur's character and its effect on the conduct of the war, see Matthew B. Ridgway, *The Korean War* (New York: Da Capo Press, 1967), chap. 6.

Chapter 7

1. An informed discussion of the problems encountered in the Congo and Lebanon missions can be found in the memoirs of Brian Urquhart, who for forty-odd years ran multiple UN missions with political astuteness, military efficiency, and a miniscule staff. See Brian Urquhart, *A Life in Peace and War* (New York: Harper and Row, 1987), p. 289, passim.

2. For Hammarskjöld's elaboration of the theory of "preventive diplomacy," see *Introduction to the Annual Report of the Secretary-General on the Work of the Organization,* June 16, 1959–June 15, 1960, GAOR, 15th session, Supp. 1A, p. 4.

3. See George L. Sherry, *The United Nations Reborn: Conflict Control in the Post–Cold War World* (New York: Council on Foreign Relations, 1990), p. 10.

4. Brian Urquhart, *Decolonization and World Peace* (Austin: The University of Texas Press, 1989), p. 57.

5. See Chester A. Crocker, *High Noon in Southern Africa: Making Peace in a Rough Neighborhood* (New York: W. W. Norton, 1992), pp. 348, 423.

6. See William J. Durch and Barry M. Blechman, *Keeping the Peace: The United Nations in the Emerging World Order* (Washington, D.C., The Henry L. Stimson Center, 1992), p. 31.

7. Crocker, *High Noon in Southern Africa*, p. 455.

8. Ibid., pp. 454–455.

9. See Mikhail Gorbachev, *Perestroika: New Thinking for Our Country and the World* (New York: Harper and Row, 1988), p. 265, on implementing the decisions of the Twenty-Seventh Congress of the Communist Party of the Soviet Union.

10. Quoted in Crocker, *High Noon in Southern Africa*, p. 348.

11. Quoted in John Tessitore and Susan Woolfson, eds., *Issues 44: Issues Before the 44th General Assembly of the United Nations* (Lexington, Mass.: D. C. Heath, 1990), p. 3.

12. See Bukar Bukarambe, "The UN Observer Force in Namibia," in *Nigeria in International Peacekeeping, 1960–1992,* edited by M. A. Vogt and A. E. Ekoko (Lagos: Malthouse Press, 1993), p. 178. It will be recalled from Chapter 2 that the League of Nations was also involved in election monitoring, most notably in the Saar plebiscite of 1935, which, as in Namibia, employed a gendarmerie unit to protect the voters and a substantial armed force (numbering 3,300 men) to maintain overall security.

13. See United Nations, *The Blue Helmets: A Review of United Nations Peace-Keeping* (New York: United Nations Department of Public Information, 1990), pp. 352–388; and Bukarambe, "The UN Observer Force," p. 179.

14. Durch and Blechman, *Keeping the Peace*, p. 23.

15. Ibid., p. 32.

16. United Nations, *The Blue Helmets*, p. 382.

17. See Major General Indar Jit Rikhye, *Strengthening UN Peacekeeping: New Challenges and Proposals* (Washington, D.C.: United States Institute of Peace, 1992), p. 13.

18. See Linda Freeman, "The Contradictions of Independence: Namibia in Transition," *International Journal* (Fall 1991), p. 690.

19. See Patrick O'Meara, review of *Namibia: The Nation After Independence*, by Donald L. Sparks and December Green, *The Journal of Developing Areas* (April 1994), p. 450.

20. See Anne-Marie Smith, *Advances in Understanding International Peacekeeping* (Washington, D.C.: United States Institute of Peace, 1997), p. 10.

21. In the late 1990s, despite the lowered expectations of peacekeeping, the Security Council considers even more issues than it did during the early years of the post–Soviet era. According to some permanent-member delegates who also served in New York during the 1970s and 1980s, the council deals with more than twice as many items as it did during the Cold War and perhaps one-third again as many as during the early 1980s. It now meets formally or informally two or three times a week on each agenda item. Most items relate to the peaceful settlement of disputes through mediation, election monitoring, and negotiation under Chapter VI rather than to economic or military enforcement action under Chapter VII.

22. See Richard Holbrooke, *To End a War* (New York: Random House, 1998), p. 112.

Chapter 8

1. This and the following paragraph draw on two addresses by Thomas R. Pickering, former U.S. permanent representative to the United Nations.

2. The trouble with this interpretation of Article 51 is that, carried to its logical conclusion, it would eviscerate the sovereign right of collective self-defense, making that right subject to Security Council permission. Since the UN Charter does not rule out concurrent jurisdiction by the council and states that are assisting a victim of aggression at its request, it seems advisable to permit such assistance so long as it does not cut across Security Council decisions. See Eugene V. Rostow, "Enforcement Action or Self-Defense?" (paper presented at a conference entitled "The Crisis in the Gulf: Enforcing the Rule of Law," sponsored by the American Bar Association, Standing Committee on Law and National Security, Washington, D.C., January 30, 1991).

3. On the controversy over this provision at San Francisco, see Leland M. Goodrich and Edvard Hambro, *Charter of the United Nations: Commentary and Documents* (Boston: World Peace Foundation, 1946), p. 171.

4. See Robert C. Hilderbrand, *Dumbarton Oaks: The Origins of the United Nations and the Search for Postwar Security* (Chapel Hill: The University of North Carolina Press, 1990), p. 157.

5. On the importance to preventive diplomacy of a graduated system of deterrents, see Brian Urquhart, "Traits of Successful Conflict Resolvers," in *Dialogues on Conflict Resolution: Bridging Theory and Practice* (Washington, D.C.: United States Institute of Peace, 1993), p. 41.

6. In the October 1973 war in the Middle East, advance elements of the UN emergency force (UNEF II) were in place, separating Israeli and Egyptian forces, within twelve hours of the Security Council's authorization of the operation. Granted, some of these units were "borrowed" from the UN peacekeeping force in Cyprus and transported by U.S. military aircraft under orders to carry out the operation as quickly as possible. The fact remains that when the political will exists, the means can be found for extraordinarily fast deployment.

Chapter 9

1. See Ruben P. Mendez, "Paying for Peace and Development," *Foreign Policy* (Fall 1995), p. 22; and Charles William Maynes, "The New Pessimism," *Foreign Policy* (Fall 1995), p. 41.

2. See Mendez, "Paying for Peace," p. 22; and Joseph S. Nye Jr., "The Self-Determination Trap," *Washington Post*, December 15, 1992.

3. General Assembly Resolution 733, January 23, 1992. This resolution is unusual from a procedural standpoint in that it singles out one of its eleven operative paragraphs as a decision taken under Chapter VII.

4. Stephen Smith, *Somalie: La guerre perdue de l'humanitaire* (Paris: Calmann-Lévy, 1993), p. 14 (my translation).

5. Walter S. Clarke, "Testing the World's Resolve in Somalia," *Parameters* (Winter 1993-1994), p. 57.

6. Hussein Adam, *Statement Before the Subcommittee on Africa*, House Committee on Foreign Affairs, U.S. Congress, February 17, 1993, p. 44.

7. Ibid.

8. See John L. Hirsch and Robert B. Oakley, *Somalia and Operation Restore Hope: Reflections on Peacemaking and Peacekeeping* (Washington, D.C.: United States Institute of Peace, 1995), pp. 3, 11–15. This balanced and informed book is the most useful analysis I have seen of what worked and what went wrong during the U.S. and UN interventions in Somalia.

9. Thomas Hobbes, *Leviathan* (London: n.p., 1651), pt. 1, chap. 13.

10. See Hirsch and Oakley, *Somalia and Operation Restore Hope*, p. 20.

11. See Jonathan Stevenson, "Hope Restored in Somalia?" *Foreign Policy* (Summer 1993), p. 149.

12. This OAU initiative was the high point of African involvement in the Somalia crisis. Henceforth "the Organization of African Unity largely ignored Somalia . . . [and] sub-Saharan Africa essentially deserted it." Stevenson, "Hope Restored in Somalia?" p. 145.

13. See Mohamed Sahnoun, *Somalia: The Missed Opportunities* (Washington, D.C.: United States Institute of Peace, 1994), pp. 5–11; and Chester A. Crocker, "The Lessons of Somalia," *Foreign Affairs* (May-June 1995), p. 6.

14. Sahnoun, *Somalia*, p. 15.

15. Security Council Resolution 751, April 24, 1992.

16. Security Council Resolution 775, August 28, 1992.

17. Security Council Resolution 767, July 27, 1992. Germany and Canada also provided airlifts after this resolution was adopted.

18. In October 1991, when the full force of the civil war hit Mogadishu, the UN moved the offices of UNICEF, the UN High Commissioner for Refugees, and the World Food Program to Nairobi. A year later, after the security situation in Mogadishu had improved, these agencies returned to the capital. See Hirsch and Oakley, *Somalia and Operation Restore Hope*, p. 18.

19. Office of U.S. Foreign Disaster Assistance (OFDA) Situation Report no. 11, August 1992.

20. In one of Mohamed Sahnoun's many broadsides against the UN's specialized agencies, leading finally to Boutros-Ghali's acceptance of his resignation, he declared to *Le Monde* that "with the exception of UNICEF, the UN agencies do not seem prepared to face hazardous situations. . . . The nongovernmental organizations, on the other hand, are made up of volunteers who agree to work in difficult conditions. Therein lies their effectiveness." Quoted in Smith, *Somalie*, p. 124 (my translation).

21. Through fiscal year 1993 the U.S. government allocated approximately 215,000 metric tons of food aid, valued at $85.5 million, for famine relief in Somalia. This represented over 65 percent of the total food aid to Somalia for that period. See the OFDA Fact Sheets dated August 10 and September 22, 1993.

22. The total airlift operation included elements from the air forces of Germany, France, Great Britain, Canada, and Belgium as well as the United States. Land and sea transport was provided by Saudi Arabia, Nigeria, and other governments and agencies.

23. Remarks in the Security Council, July 23, 1992, *Facts on File*, vol. 52, no. 2700, p. 623.

24. The resolution was adopted as S. Con. Res. 132, August 10, 1992.

25. Sahnoun, *Somalia*, p. 18.

26. Ibid.

27. Quoted in Sahnoun, *Somalia*, pp. 17–18.

28. OFDA Situation Report no. 11, August 1992.

29. Sahnoun, *Somalia*, p. 20.

30. Pierre Pont, Head of Delegation for North America, ICRC Washington Delegation, conversation with author, July 1996. The ICRC lost two more delegates during the first three months after UNITAF's arrival. Indeed, casualties increased throughout the relief community at this time as "relief workers, valued by gunmen before Operation Restore Hope as a source of semi-legitimate 'protection' income, [became] prime targets for armed robbery. During [this period] three expatriate aid workers were killed, compared to only two during the preceding two years of anarchy." Stevenson, "Hope Restored in Somalia?" p. 139.

31. On the ICRC's ground rules for the distribution of relief in conflict situations and its practices in Somalia, see Smith, *Somalie*, pp. 105–109. But see also Hirsch and Oakley, *Somalia and Operation Restore Hope*, p. 25.

32. See Sahnoun, *Somalia*, p. 29.

33. See House Subcommittee on Africa, *Recent Developments in Somalia: Testimony of Deputy Assistant Secretary of State for African Affairs Robert Houdek*, 103rd Congress, 1st session, February 17, 1993, p. 3.

34. NATO commanders in the field have made line troops available for the arrest of war criminals, but have been reluctant to do so without a broadened mandate from the Security Council. See, for example, the comments of General George A. Joulwan, the U.S. commander of ITAF and its successor force, quoted in *New York Times*, December 18, 1996. For an account of the controversy between U.S. military and diplomatic officials on the arrest of war criminals in Bosnia, see Richard Holbrooke, *To End a War* (New York: Random House, 1998), pp. 226, 250, 329.

35. Sahnoun, *Somalia*, p. 27.

36. Ibid., p. 32.

37. Stevenson, "Hope Restored in Somalia?" p. 152.

38. Smith, *Somalie*, p. 156.

39. Sahnoun, *Somalia*, p. 53.

40. Ibid., p. 43.

41. Robert B. Oakley, "A Diplomatic Perspective on African Conflict Resolution," in *African Conflict Resolution: The U.S. Role in Peacemaking*, edited by David R. Smock and Chester A. Crocker (Washington, D.C.: United States Institute of Peace, 1995), p. 68.

42. Hirsch and Oakley, *Somalia and Operation Restore Hope*, p. 25.

43. OFDA Situation Report no. 9, May 1992.

44. OFDA Situation Reports nos. 10–18, June 1992–January 1993.

45. OFDA Situation Reports nos. 19–20, February–March 1993.

46. Office of Public Affairs, Office of the Secretary of Defense, Department of Defense, in response to my inquiry. The figure is through fiscal year 1994.

47. OFDA Fact Sheet dated September 22, 1993.

48. Ricky Gold, OFDA, Bureau for Food and Humanitarian Assistance, Agency for International Assistance.

49. Dina Esposito, OFDA, Bureau for Food and Humanitarian Assistance, Agency for International Assistance.

50. Andrew Kohut and Robert Toth, "Arms and the People," *Foreign Affairs* (November-December 1994), p. 51.

51. Ibid., p. 53.

52. Ibid., p. 52.

53. Jonathan T. Howe, "The United States and the United Nations in Somalia," *The Washington Quarterly* (Summer 1995), p. 55.

54. Eliot A. Cohen, "Recent Books," *Foreign Affairs* (July-August 1995), p. 138.

55. Hirsch and Oakley, *Somalia and Operation Restore Hope*, p. 159.

56. Crocker, "The Lessons of Somalia," p. 7.

57. The definition of aggression adopted by the General Assembly in 1974 with U.S. support includes among the criteria "the use of force against the . . . political

independence" of another state—a succinct description of Serbia's intervention in Bosnia. See General Assembly Resolution 3314(XXIX), December 14, 1974.

58. Leslie H. Gelb, "Quelling the Teacup Wars," *Foreign Affairs* (November-December 1994), p. 5.

59. See Kenneth Allard, *Somalia Operations: Lessons Learned* (Washington, D.C.: National Defense University Press, 1995), p. 60. In this U.S. military postmortem of the Somalia missions, Allard remarks that "the greatest obstacles to unity of command during UNOSOM II were imposed by the United States on itself."

60. As an example of this debate, see Michael Mandelbaum, "Foreign Policy As Social Work," *Foreign Affairs* (January-February 1996), pp. 16–32; and Stanley Hoffmann, "In Defense of Mother Teresa," *Foreign Affairs* (March-April 1996), pp. 172–175.

61. Conversations with representatives of permanent-member missions in New York, February 1997 and January 1998.

62. Quoted in *New York Times,* December 18, 1996.

63. Allard, *Somalia Operations,* p. 61.

64. Boutros Boutros-Ghali, *An Agenda for Peace* (New York: United Nations, 1992), p. 26.

65. Boutros Boutros-Ghali, *An Agenda for Peace 1995* (New York: United Nations, 1995), para. 77. This paragraph was added to *An Agenda for Peace* when it was reissued in January 1995.

66. See Thomas G. Weiss, David P. Forsythe, and Roger A. Coate, *The United Nations and Changing World Politics,* 2nd ed. (Boulder: Westview Press, 1997), p. 100.

Chapter 10

1. See Brian Urquhart, "For a Volunteer UN Force," *The New York Review of Books* (June 10, 1993), pp. 3–4, and the following two issues of the same periodical (June 24 and July 15), which carry a discussion of Urquhart's ideas by Lee Hamilton, Gareth Evans, Field Marshall Lord Carver, Stanley Hoffmann, Robert Oakley, and McGeorge Bundy. Also, in similar proposals, arguments for a powerful, fast-reaction UN force drawn from the military powers can be found in Richard N. Gardner, "Collective Security and the 'New World Order,'" in *Two Views on the Issue of Collective Security,* by Richard N. Gardner and Joseph P. Lorenz (Washington, D.C.: United States Institute of Peace, 1992), pp. 9–16; and David H. Popper, "The Future of the Coalition" (paper presented at a meeting of the American Academy of Diplomacy, Washington, D.C., June 12, 1991), pp. 7–10.

2. Urquhart, "For a Volunteer UN Force," p. 4.

Bibliography

Acheson, Dean. "Oral Report Delivered Before the Political and Security Committee of the United Nations General Assembly on October 24, 1952." Department of State Publication 4771. Washington, D.C.: U.S. Government Printing Office, 1952.

_____. *Present at the Creation: My Years in the State Department.* New York: W. W. Norton, 1969.

Adam, Hussein. *Statement Before the Subcommittee on Africa,* House Committee on Foreign Affairs, U.S. Congress, February 17, 1993.

Allard, Kenneth. *Somalia Operations: Lessons Learned.* Washington, D.C.: National Defense University Press, 1995.

Aron, Raymond. *Le Grand Schisme.* Paris: Gallimard, 1948.

_____. "Limits to the Powers of the United Nations," *Annals of the American Academy of Political and Social Sciences* (November 1954).

_____. *The Dawn of Universal History.* New York: Praeger, 1961.

_____. *Le Grand Débat. Initiation à la stratégie atomique.* Paris: Calmann-Lévy, 1962.

_____. *Paix et Guerre entre les nations.* Paris: Calmann-Lévy, 1962.

_____. *Main Currents in Sociological Thought.* London: Pelican Books, 1968.

_____. *The Imperial Republic: The United States and the World 1945–1973.* New York: University Press of America, 1974.

_____. *La Guerre froide. Les articles de politique internationale dans Le Figaro de 1947 à 1977.* Paris: Éditions de Fallois, 1990.

Attlee, Clement R. *Collective Security Under the United Nations.* London: The David Davies Memorial Institute of International Studies, 1958.

Blaisdell, Donald C. *Arms for the United Nations.* Washington, D.C.: U.S. Department of State, 1948.

Boutros-Ghali, Boutros. *An Agenda for Peace.* New York: United Nations, 1992.

_____. *An Agenda for Peace 1995.* New York: United Nations, 1995.

Bukarambe, Bukar. "The UN Observer Force in Namibia." In *Nigeria in International Peacekeeping, 1960–1992,* edited by M. A. Vogt and A. E. Ekoko. Lagos: Malthouse Press, 1993.

Clarke, Walter S. "Testing the World's Resolve in Somalia." *Parameters* (Winter 1993–1994).

Claude, Inis L., Jr. "The United Nations and the Use of Force." *International Conciliation* (March 1961).

_____. *Power and International Relations.* New York: Random House, 1962.

_____. *Swords into Plowshares: The Problems and Progress of International Organization.* 3rd ed. New York: Random House, 1964.

_____. "Implications and Questions for the Future." In *The United Nations in the Balance,* edited by Norman J. Padelford and Leland M. Goodrich. New York: Praeger, 1965.

Cleveland, Harlan. "The Evolution of Rising Responsibility." In *The United Nations in the Balance,* edited by Norman J. Padelford and Leland M. Goodrich. New York: Praeger, 1965.

Cohen, Eliot A. "Recent Books." *Foreign Affairs* (July-August 1995).

Craig, Gordon A., and Alexander L. George. *Force and Statecraft: Diplomatic Problems of Our Time.* New York: Oxford University Press, 1983.

Crocker, Chester A. *High Noon in Southern Africa: Making Peace in a Rough Neighborhood.* New York: W. W. Norton, 1992.

_____. "The Lessons of Somalia." *Foreign Affairs* (May-June 1995).

Durch, William J. and Blechman, Barry M. *Keeping the Peace: The United Nations in the Emerging World Order.* Washington, D.C.: The Henry L. Stimson Center, 1992.

Eagleton, Clyde, and Richard N. Swift, eds. *Annual Review of United Nations Affairs, 1950.* New York: New York University Press, 1951.

Evans, Gareth. "A UN Volunteer Military Force: Four Views." *The New York Review of Books* (June 24, 1993).

Foley, Hamilton. *Woodrow Wilson's Case for the League of Nations.* Princeton: Princeton University Press, 1923.

Frankenstein, Marc. "Les initiatives de l'Inde pour le règlement du conflit coréen." *Revue Politique et Parlementaire* (July 1951).

Freeman, Linda. "The Contradictions of Independence: Namibia in Transition." *International Journal* (Fall 1991).

Gardner, Richard N. "Collective Security and the 'New World Order.'" In *Two Views on the Issue of Collective Security,* by Richard N. Gardner and Joseph P. Lorenz. Washington, D.C.: United States Institute of Peace, 1992.

Gelb, Leslie H. "Quelling the Teacup Wars." *Foreign Affairs* (November-December 1994).

General Assembly, Official Records. *Introduction to the Annual Report of the Secretary-General on the Work of the Organization.* 15th session, Supp. 1A, June 16, 1959–June 15, 1960.

Goodrich, Leland M. "Korea: Collective Measures Against Aggression." *International Conciliation* (October 1953).

_____. *Korea: A Study of U.S. Policy in the United Nations.* New York: Council on Foreign Relations, 1956.

_____. *The United Nations.* New York: Crowell, 1959.

_____. *The United Nations in a Changing World.* New York: Columbia University Press, 1974.

Goodrich, Leland M., and Edvard Hambro. *Charter of the United Nations: Commentary and Documents.* Boston: World Peace Foundation, 1946.

Goodrich, Leland M., and Anne P. Simons. *The United Nations and the Maintenance of International Peace and Security.* Washington, D.C.: The Brookings Institution, 1955.

Goodspeed, Stephen S. *The Nature and Function of International Organization.* 2nd ed. New York: Oxford University Press, 1967.

Gorbachev, Mikhail. *Perestroika: New Thinking for Our Country and the World.* New York: Harper and Row, 1988.

Haas, Ernst B., and Allen S. Whiting. *Dynamics of International Relations.* New York: McGraw-Hill, 1956.

Hilderbrand, Robert C. *Dumbarton Oaks: The Origins of the United Nations and the Search for Postwar Security.* Chapel Hill: The University of North Carolina Press, 1990.

Hirsch, John L., and Robert B. Oakley. *Somalia and Operation Restore Hope: Reflections on Peacemaking and Peacekeeping.* Washington, D.C.: United States Institute of Peace, 1995.

Hobbes, Thomas. *Leviathan.* London: n.p., 1651.

Hoffmann, Stanley. "Obstinate or Obsolete? The Fate of the Nation-State and the Case of Modern Europe." In *Conditions of World Order,* edited by Stanley Hoffmann. Boston: Houghton Mifflin, 1968.

_____. *Primacy or World Order: American Foreign Policy Since the Cold War.* New York: McGraw-Hill, 1978.

_____. "The Future of the International Political System: A Sketch." In *Global Dilemmas,* edited by Samuel P. Huntington and Joseph S. Nye. Cambridge, Mass.: Center for International Affairs, 1985.

_____. "In Defense of Mother Teresa." *Foreign Affairs* (March-April 1996).

Holbrooke, Richard. *To End a War.* New York: Random House, 1998.

Hoopes, Towsend, and Douglas Brinkley. *FDR and the Creation of the U.N.* New Haven: Yale University Press, 1997.

House Subcommittee on Africa. *Recent Developments in Somalia: Testimony of Deputy Assistant Secretary of State for African Affairs Robert Houdek,* 103rd Congress, 1st session, February 17, 1993.

Howe, Jonathan T. "The United States and the United Nations in Somalia." *The Washington Quarterly* (Summer 1995).

Huntington, Samuel. *The Clash of Civilizations and the Remaking of the World Order.* New York: Simon & Schuster, 1996.

Jervis, Robert. "From Balance to Concert: A Study of International Security Cooperation." *World Politics* (October 1985).

Joyce, James Avery. *Broken Star: The Story of the League of Nations, 1919–1939.* Swansea: Christopher Davies, 1975.

Kennan, George F. "The Sources of Soviet Conduct." *Foreign Affairs* (Spring 1987). Reprinted from *Foreign Affairs* (July 1947).

_____. "Foreign Aid in the Framework of National Policy." In *Principles and Problems of International Politics,* edited by Hans J. Morgenthau and Kenneth W. Thompson. New York: Knopf, 1952.

_____. "Is War with Russia Inevitable?" In *Principles and Problems of International Politics,* edited by Hans J. Morgenthau and Kenneth W. Thompson. New York: Knopf, 1952.

_____. *Russia, the Atom and the West.* New York: Harper, 1957.

_____. *Memoirs, 1925–1950.* Boston: Little, Brown, 1967.

_____. *Around the Cragged Hill.* New York: W. W. Norton, 1993.

Keohane, Robert O., and Joseph S. Nye. *Power and Interdependence: World Politics in Transition.* Boston: Little, Brown, 1977.

_____. "Power and Interdependence Revisited." *International Organization* (Autumn 1987).

Kissinger, Henry A. *Nuclear Weapons and Foreign Policy*. New York: Harper, 1957.

_____. *The Necessity for Choice*. Garden City, N.Y.: Doubleday, 1962.

_____. "Domestic Structure and Foreign Policy." In *Conditions of World Order*, edited by Stanley Hoffmann. Boston: Houghton Mifflin, 1968.

_____. "False Dreams of a New World Order." *Washington Post*, February 26, 1991.

_____. *Diplomacy*. New York: Simon and Schuster, 1994.

Kohut, Andrew, and Robert Toth. "Arms and the People." *Foreign Affairs* (November-December 1994).

Larus, Joel. *From Collective Security to Preventive Diplomacy*. New York: John Wiley, 1965.

Lie, Trygve. *In the Cause of Peace*. New York: Macmillan, 1954.

Lippmann, Walter. *Essays in the Public Philosophy*. Boston: Little, Brown, 1955.

Luard, Evan. *Conflict and Peace in the Modern International System*. Boston: Little, Brown, 1968.

_____. *A History of the United Nations: The Years of Western Domination, 1945–1955*. New York: St. Martin's Press, 1982.

Mandelbaum, Michael. "Foreign Policy As Social Work." *Foreign Affairs* (January-February 1996).

Maynes, Charles William. "The New Pessimism." *Foreign Policy* (Fall 1995).

Mendez, Ruben P. "Paying for Peace and Development." *Foreign Policy* (Fall 1995).

Miller, Lynn H. *Global Order: Values and Power in International Politics*. Boulder: Westview Press, 1990.

Morgenthau, Hans J. *Politics Among Nations: The Struggle for Power and Peace*. 5th ed. New York: Knopf, 1973.

_____. *A New Foreign Policy for the United States*. New York: Praeger, 1969.

Morgenthau, Hans J., ed. *Peace, Security, and the United Nations*. Chicago: The University of Chicago Press, 1946.

Morgenthau, Hans J., and Kenneth W. Thompson, eds. *Principles and Problems of International Politics*. New York: Knopf, 1952.

Moynihan, Daniel Patrick. *A Dangerous Place*. Boston: Little, Brown, 1975.

Nicolson, Harold. *Diaries and Letters*. Vol. 1, *1930–1939*. Edited by Nigel Nicolson. New York: Atheneum, 1966.

_____. *Diaries and Letters*. Vol. 2, *The War Years, 1939–1945*. Edited by Nigel Nicolson. New York: Atheneum, 1967.

Oakley, Robert B. "A Diplomatic Perspective on African Conflict Resolution." In *African Conflict Resolution: The U.S. Role in Peacemaking*, edited by David R. Smock and Chester A. Crocker. Washington, D.C.: United States Institute of Peace, 1995.

O'Meara, Patrick. Review of *Namibia: The Nation After Independence*, by Donald L. Sparks and December Green. *The Journal of Developing Areas* (April 1994).

Ostrower, Gary B. *Collective Insecurity: The United States and the League of Nations During the Early Thirties*. Lewisburg, Pa.: Bucknell University Press, 1979.

Plano, Jack C., and Robert E. Riggs. *Forging World Order: The Politics of International Organization.* New York: Macmillan, 1967.

Popper, David H. "The Future of the Coalition." Paper presented at a meeting of the American Academy of Diplomacy, Washington, D.C., June 12, 1991.

Ridgway, Matthew B. *The Korean War.* New York: Da Capo Press, 1967.

Riggs, Robert E., and Jack C. Plano. *The United Nations: International Organization and World Politics.* Chicago: The Dorsey Press, 1988.

Rikhye, Indar Jit. *Strengthening UN Peacekeeping: New Challenges and Proposals.* Washington, D.C.: United States Institute of Peace, 1992.

Rostow, Eugene V. "Enforcement Action or Self-Defense?" Paper presented at a conference entitled "The Crisis in the Gulf: Enforcing the Rule of Law," sponsored by the American Bar Association, Standing Committee on Law and National Security, Washington, D.C., January 30, 1991.

Russell, Ruth B. *A History of the United Nations Charter: The Role of the United States 1940–1945.* Washington, D.C.: The Brookings Institution, 1958.

Russett, Bruce, and James S. Sutterlin. "The U.N. in a New World Order." *Foreign Affairs* (Spring 1991).

Sahnoun, Mohamed. *Somalia: The Missed Opportunities.* Washington, D.C.: United States Institute of Peace, 1994.

Senate Committees on Armed Services and Foreign Relations. *Hearings to Conduct an Inquiry into the Military Situation in the Far East and the Facts Surrounding the Relief of General of the Army Douglas MacArthur from His Assignments in That Area.* 82nd Congress, 1st session. Washington, D.C.: U.S. Government Printing Office, 1951.

Sherry, George L. *The United Nations Reborn: Conflict Control in the Post–Cold War World.* New York: Council on Foreign Relations, 1990.

Smith, Anne-Marie. *Advances in Understanding International Peacekeeping.* Washington, D.C.: United States Institute of Peace, 1997.

Smith, Stephen. *Somalie: La guerre perdue de l'humanitaire.* Paris: Calmann-Lévy, 1993.

Spykman, Nicholas J. *The Geography of the Peace.* New York: Harcourt, Brace, 1944.

Stevenson, Jonathan. "Hope Restored in Somalia?" *Foreign Policy* (Summer 1993).

Stoessinger, John G. "The Statesman and the Critic: Kissinger and Morgenthau." In *A Tribute to Hans Morgenthau,* edited by Kenneth W. Thompson and Robert Myers. Washington, D.C.: The New Republic Book Company, 1977.

Syed, Anwar Hussain. *Walter Lippmann's Philosophy of International Politics.* Philadelphia: The University of Pennsylvania Press, 1963.

Taylor, A. J. P. *English History, 1914–1945.* New York: Oxford University Press, 1965.

Tessitore, John, and Susan Woolfson. *Issues 44: Issues Before the 44th General Assembly of the United Nations.* Lexington, Mass.: D. C. Heath, 1990.

Thompson, Kenneth W. *Political Realism and the Crisis of World Politics: An American Approach to Foreign Policy.* Princeton: Princeton University Press, 1960.

United Nations. "Report on General Principles Governing the Organization of the Armed Forces to Be Made Available to the Security Council by Member Nations of the United Nations." In *Yearbook of the United Nations 1946–1947.* Lake Success, N.Y.: United Nations Department of Public Information, 1947.

_____. *The Blue Helmets: A Review of United Nations Peace-Keeping.* New York: United Nations Department of Public Information, 1990.

Urquhart, Brian. *A Life in Peace and War.* New York: Harper and Row, 1987.

_____. *Decolonization and World Peace.* Austin: The University of Texas Press, 1989.

_____. "Traits of Successful Conflict Resolvers." In *Dialogues on Conflict Resolution: Bridging Theory and Practice.* Washington, D.C.: United States Institute of Peace, 1993.

_____. "For a Volunteer UN Force." *The New York Review of Books* (June 10, 1993).

U.S. Department of State. *Foreign Relations of the United States, 1946.* Vol. 1, *General: The United Nations.* Washington, D.C.: U.S. Government Printing Office, 1972.

Vandenberg, Arthur H., Jr., ed. *The Private Papers of Senator Vandenberg.* Boston: Houghton Mifflin, 1952.

Warren, Charles. "Congress and Neutrality." In *Neutrality and Collective Security,* edited by Quincy Wright. Chicago: The University of Chicago Press, 1936.

Weiss, Thomas G., Forsythe, David P., and Coate, Roger A. *The United Nations and Changing World Politics.* 2nd ed. Boulder: Westview Press, 1997.

Yoo, Tae-Ho. *The Korean War and the United Nations: A Legal and Diplomatic Study.* Louvain, France: Université Catholique de Louvain, 1964.

Zimmern, Sir Alfred. "The Problem of Collective Security." In *Neutrality and Collective Security,* edited by Quincy Wright. Chicago: The University of Chicago Press, 1936.

Index